100-DAY LEADERS

Turning Short-Term Wins Into
Long-Term Success in Schools

DOUGLAS REEVES · ROBERT EAKER
FOREWORD BY MICHAEL FULLAN

Solution Tree | Press

555 North Morton Street
Bloomington, IN 47404
800.733.6786 (toll free) / 812.336.7700
FAX: 812.336.7790

email: info@SolutionTree.com
SolutionTree.com

Visit **go.SolutionTree.com/leadership** to download the free reproducibles in this book.

Printed in the United States of America

Library of Congress Cataloging-in-Publication Data

Names: Eaker, Robert E., author. | Reeves, Douglas B., 1953- author.
Title: 100-day leaders : turning short-term wins into long-term success in
    schools / Robert Eaker and Douglas Reeves.
Description: Bloomington, IN : Solution Tree Press, [2019] | Includes
    bibliographical references and index.
Identifiers: LCCN 2018060840 | ISBN 9781949539257 (perfect bound)
Subjects: LCSH: Educational leadership--United States. | Educational
    change--United States.
Classification: LCC LB2805 .E1995 2019 | DDC 371.2--dc23 LC record available at
    https://lccn.loc.gov/2018060840

Solution Tree
Jeffrey C. Jones, CEO
Edmund M. Ackerman, President

Solution Tree Press
President and Publisher: Douglas M. Rife
Associate Publisher: Sarah Payne-Mills
Art Director: Rian Anderson
Managing Production Editor: Kendra Slayton
Senior Production Editor: Suzanne Kraszewski
Content Development Specialist: Amy Rubenstein
Copy Editor: Jessi Finn
Proofreader: Evie Madsen
Text and Cover Designer: Abigail Bowen
Editorial Assistant: Sarah Ludwig

For Rick and Becky

This book is dedicated to my dear friend
Douglas Rife. Douglas has not only
enhanced the quality of my professional
life, he has been an unwavering
supporter and friend.

—Bob Eaker

ACKNOWLEDGMENTS

Although writing can be a solitary endeavor, publishing a book is a team effort. I am indebted to the team at Solution Tree Press for their collaboration and support. In particular, Suzanne Kraszewski helped shepherd this book from concept to reality. Douglas Rife and Jeff Jones have been the best of partners and friends. Michael Fullan publishes, by my rough count, a book after every meal, and yet found the time to write a very gracious foreword for this one. He is a model colleague and great friend. Bob Eaker is an inspiration to me and to educators and leaders around the world. His gentle wit, compassion, and commitment to education represent the best of our profession.

—Douglas Reeves

For twenty years, Jeff Jones has been a personal friend and a constant source of encouragement and caring. This book, as well as so many of my other projects, simply would not have happened without Jeff's constant support. And, this particular book would not have become a reality without the friendship and intellectual insights of Doug Reeves. Doug represents the best our profession has to offer, and his friendship and initiative with this book is very much appreciated.

—Robert Eaker

Solution Tree Press would like to thank the following reviewers:

Rob Bueche
Executive Director of
    Federal Programs and
    School Innovation
Humboldt Unified
    School District
Prescott Valley, Arizona

Bill Hall
Solution Tree Associate
Melbourne, Florida

Molly Large
Chancellor
Edwin Rhodes
    Elementary School
Chino, California

Bruce Preston
Assistant Superintendent of
    Curriculum & Personnel
Howell Township
    Public Schools
Howell, New Jersey

Bo Ryan
Principal
Greater Hartford Academy of
    the Arts Middle School
Hartford, Connecticut

Kim Timmerman
Principal
Adel Desoto Minburn
    Middle School
Adel, Iowa

Suzan Watkins
Principal
Dr. Martin Luther King Jr.
    Elementary School
Macon, Georgia

Steven Weber
Associate Superintendent for
    Teaching and Learning
Fayetteville Public Schools
Fayetteville, Arkansas

TABLE OF CONTENTS

Reproducibles are in italics.

PART 2

Creating the Environment for Success 71

ABOUT THE AUTHORS

 **DOUGLAS REEVES, PhD,** is the author of more than thirty books and many articles about leadership and organizational effectiveness. He was named the Brock International Laureate for his contributions to education and received the Contribution to the Field Award from the National Staff Development Council (now Learning Forward). Dr. Reeves has addressed audiences in all fifty U.S. states and more than thirty countries, sharing his research and supporting effective leadership at the local, state, and national levels. He is founder of Finish the Dissertation, a free and noncommercial service for doctoral students, and the Zambian Leadership and Learning Institute. He is the founding editor and copublisher of *The SNAFU Review*, a collection of essays, poetry, and art by veterans suffering from post-traumatic stress disorder. Dr. Reeves lives with his family in downtown Boston.

To learn more about the work of Dr. Reeves, visit Creative Leadership Solutions at https://creativeleadership.net, or follow @DouglasReeves on Twitter.

 **ROBERT EAKER, EdD,** is professor emeritus at Middle Tennessee State University, where he also served as dean of the College of Education and later as interim executive vice president and provost. Dr. Eaker is a former fellow with the National Center for Effective Schools Research and Development.

Dr. Eaker has written widely on the issues of effective teaching, effective schools, helping teachers use research findings, and high expectations for student achievement, and has coauthored (with Richard and Rebecca DuFour) numerous books and other resources on the topic of reculturing schools and school districts into professional learning communities (PLCs).

In 1998, Dr. Eaker was recognized by the governor of Tennessee as a recipient of Tennessee's Outstanding Achievement Award. Also, in 1998, the Tennessee House of Representatives passed a proclamation recognizing him for his dedication and commitment to the field of education. In 2003, Dr. Eaker was selected by the Middle Tennessee State University Student Government Association to receive the Womack Distinguished Faculty Award.

For over four decades, Dr. Eaker has served as a consultant to school districts throughout North America and has been a frequent speaker at state, regional, and national meetings.

To learn more about Dr. Eaker's work, visit AllThingsPLC (www.allthingsplc.info).

To book Douglas Reeves or Robert Eaker for professional development, contact pd@SolutionTree.com.

FOREWORD

By Michael Fullan

IN THE 1980s, I said that systemic change in schools and districts requires five to seven years of work. Now we know that change can happen at a much faster pace. Since then, research has shown that leaders armed with practical knowledge and partnering within their communities can achieve remarkable changes within a year or two. (See Fullan and Pinchot [2018] for a case of powerful change in culture within a year.) Douglas Reeves and Robert Eaker, in this excellent resource, provide a framework for how leaders can establish success within one hundred days. Few books combine moral purpose and practical success so readily.

Reeves and Eaker begin by showing leaders how to strip away the superfluous distractions, and what to specifically focus on to get results. They smartly observe if a seven-year-old can't explain your mission statement, then you are in trouble. Readers quickly discover not only how to establish the right values but also how to "clear the decks" with an initiative inventory in which leaders take a hard look at what initiatives are underway so as to identify those that are the most critical.

Reeves and Eaker supply strategies and tools to help leaders get on course and stay there. After clearing the decks, leaders find out about the importance of keeping a not-to-do list. Reeves and Eaker follow with guidelines that support the leader each step of the way to short-term wins: defining high-leverage practices, assessing specific results, energizing people with what matters most, breaking down the hundred days into doable chunks, and ensuring accountability and persistence. They advocate collaboration where it counts to leverage their practical ideas. And they provide an account of what effective collaboration looks like in practice, ensuring—not just encouraging—collaboration; creating a shared understanding of teamwork; and building aligned teams districtwide to get continuous results.

Reeves and Eaker have written a powerful and inspirational resource. My recommendation is that, before reading *100-Day Leaders*, you take a moment to reflect on the following questions.

- Do I find myself doing things that don't have much of a positive impact?
- How energetic and focused are those in my organization?
- Are we getting anywhere?
- What results can I point to?
- What can I do in the short term to change things for the better?

Now you are ready to benefit from this practical and thorough book on leadership. Take a hundred days at a time, and follow the lead of these two authors who combine more than a century of practical leadership experience in these pages. They share the wisdom they have collected by working with hundreds of leaders who have found their way one hundred days at a time.

INTRODUCTION

WHY ONE HUNDRED DAYS?

IN OUR TRAVELS around the world presenting at educational conferences and consulting with schools, we have noticed that too many educational leaders are experiencing frustration, fragmentation, and burnout. They face more demands than ever before, yet they have the same amount of time they have always had—just twenty-four hours in a day—to get the job done. Many leaders are overwhelmed with priorities, projects, and tasks and feel like they are in an endless game of whack-a-mole, attempting to hit every demand that arises, while not making progress on their most important priorities. Although leaders can't add hours to the day, they can make every hour more productive and focused. If you have felt the frustration of too many demands on your time and a horizon full of things to get done, then this book is for you.

In this book, we present a system for focusing on the highest-leverage leadership actions that will yield significant results in just one hundred days. Most importantly, this first one hundred days will set the pattern for the one hundred days after that, and for every succeeding one hundred days, as long as the leader bears responsibility for personal and organizational results. Our focus on short-term wins will energize your colleagues, students, and communities. While you will always have longer-term goals, this 100-day plan will provide the organizational focus and psychological energy that people in your school or district require to know that you are making progress. This plan allows you to steadily encourage and support the teachers and

1

2 | 100-DAY LEADERS

administrators in your building or district who will get the job done. You will replace the cynicism often associated with long-term strategic planning with a laser-like focus on what matters most.

If you think that one hundred days is not long enough to produce significant change, consider these remarkable accomplishments that people have achieved within that time frame: the writing of the U.S. Constitution, the longest-surviving governing document in the world, in the 18th century (Walenta, 2010); in the 19th century, Fyodor Dostoyevsky's *The Gambler* (Hoey, 2017); and the presidential and legislative enactments that lifted the United States from the Great Depression and set the stage for saving the world from fascism in the 20th century (Alter, 2006). Great things can happen in one hundred days!

Our observations of effective school change confirm these lessons from history. In a single semester—usually about one hundred days—schools have achieved dramatically improved student performance, better climate and culture, improved faculty morale, and better discipline and attendance. Our research conducted in schools around the world and published here for the first time, demonstrates that schools can do the following, within one hundred days.

- Reduce the failure rate by more than 90 percent.
- Reduce chronic absenteeism by more than 80 percent.
- Reduce the suspension rate by more than 50 percent.
- Radically transform faculty morale.

We have witnessed these results in elementary, middle, and high schools. They occur in urban, suburban, and rural schools; in schools with high concentrations of students from low-income families and schools where the students are affluent; and in schools where large numbers of students do not speak English at home and schools where the entire student body consists of native English speakers (DuFour,

DuFour, Eaker, & Many, 2010; Reeves, 2001, 2016b). These results happen among students with a wide range of demographic characteristics. If we have learned anything in more than a century of combined leadership experience, it is that leadership makes the difference for student achievement and educational equity. Although most of our experience is in the K–12 public education field, we also have leadership experience in universities, private schools, charter schools, nonprofit organizations, and the military. Regardless of the setting, we see a consistent theme: short-term wins—gains in confidence that occur within one hundred days—establish the confidence and credibility necessary for long-term success. We acknowledge the value of longer-term goals and strategies; however, we find that those have no chance of successful implementation without the momentum that results from 100-day leadership.

Years-long strategic plans that offer more platitudes than substance make stakeholders weary. What these stakeholders—parents, students, teachers, community members, and educational policymakers—long for are results. They want short-term wins that restore confidence that the hard work teachers and students engage in will yield something more than vague promises of reform.

This book suggests a new way of thinking about leadership. Whether the project is large in scope, such as transforming a school into a professional learning community (PLC; DuFour, DuFour, Eaker, Many, & Mattos, 2016), or smaller in scope, such as developing formative assessments or new grading practices in a single semester, *100-Day Leaders* brings a sense of daily accomplishment, from the classroom to the boardroom. The approach is rigorous, clearly distinguishing between implementation that is *PLC lite* (DuFour & Reeves, 2016) and the courageous, risky, and often unpopular decisions involved in implementing effective and lasting change.

We wish to make it clear what this book is and what it is not. In this book, we offer an integrated approach in which the leader will see connections that others in the organization may not find apparent; curriculum, assessment, facilities, transportation, food service, teacher evaluation, board relationships, and a host of other complex interactions lie at the heart of *100-Day Leaders*. Therefore, this book is not a policy manual, academic treatise, or checklist. Rather, it is a practical guide for leaders at every level—from state, provincial, and national policymakers to superintendents, principals, and department and grade-level team leaders—that will support immediate transformations in culture, practice, and performance. We provide a coaching and development model for leaders who are willing to challenge themselves and their leadership teams to rise to greater heights of effectiveness.

In the chapters that follow, we begin with the moral imperative of leadership. This is the fundamental obligation educators owe to the students they serve. Educators pursue this moral obligation through the PLC process, the central organizational system for effective educational organizations, from the classroom to the boardroom. We make a compelling case for the PLC process in which we share evidence of the impact that it has on student achievement.

Every leader aims to create personal and organizational change that results in continuous improvement, but successful and sustainable change is often elusive. Change begins not with hierarchical commands, but with effective introspection. Leaders cannot seek to change others until they gain the self-awareness to change themselves. Effective 100-day leaders must focus on a few priorities; our research suggests that focused leaders have dramatically more impact on student results than leaders who are fragmented due to initiative fatigue (Reeves, 2011b; Schmoker, 2011).

We then turn our attention to *culture*—the daily actions that represent what great organizations are all about. Culture is not about attitudes, words, or beliefs; rather, it is about specifically observable actions. Although leaders must see the big picture, they also understand the details of implementation, team by team, task by task, kid by kid, and skill by skill.

Leaders face myriad decisions and challenges. We suggest a disciplined approach to leadership decision making in which leaders systematically compare the advantages and disadvantages of alternatives they face. Accountability systems have, since the passage of the No Child Left Behind Act in 2001, focused on student test scores (DuFour, Reeves, & DuFour, 2018). This change was prompted, on the one hand, by frustration with lagging student achievement, and, on the other, by the recognition that a focus on "accountability" was a political asset. We suggest a system in which leaders consider not only the effects of effective education but also the causes—the factors over which leaders have the greatest influence. Persistence and resilience are two of the greatest assets of 100-day leaders, and we consider the factors that can encourage—or undermine—resilience and persistence in the face of adversity. Finally, we consider how great leaders collaborate. Although leading can be lonely and isolating, the most successful 100-day leaders engage in remarkably effective collaboration.

Following is a guide to how we've organized this two-part book.

Part 1: Exploring 100-Day Leadership

In part 1 of this book, we consider the *why* and *how* of 100-day leadership. We begin by exploring the moral imperative of leadership and then we look at the six steps to becoming a 100-day leader.

The Moral Imperative

The moral imperative to improve student learning—*why* educators do what they do—is essential, as educators will not implement prescriptions based on policy; they must see that they operate in a moral context. Moral imperatives guide our decision making when no one is looking. There are no rewards or sanctions, only a response to the leader's inner compass that provides the moral foundation for his or her decisions. Everyone in any organization, whether it is a for-profit, nonprofit, educational, military, or any other organization, must not just understand how he or she fits in functionally but also have his or her own sense of purpose within the context of the organization's mission and values. Custodial staff do not merely sweep floors; they create safe and healthy learning environments in which students can take pride. Teachers do not merely deliver content; they nurture curiosity, kindness, relationships, and lifelong learning habits. Principals do not merely set schedules and handle discipline; they guard the values that guide thousands of daily actions for everyone in the school. The moral imperative should be the focus of the opening and closing of every meeting.

The Six Steps

This book outlines six steps for implementing your 100-day leadership plan. These steps are not one-and-done actions; rather, they require review with every 100-day planning cycle. Leaders use them to create and achieve short-term wins that combine to form long-term success.

Step 1: Identify Your Values

Begin with values—your bone-deep beliefs that will prescribe the goals you will, and will not, pursue as a leader.

Step 2: Take an Initiative Inventory

List the leadership and instructional initiatives that your school already has in place. The list is always longer than you think it will be. Take an initiative inventory of everything on your plate. Ask teachers and staff about their perceptions of the initiatives. Two key questions leaders should ask are, "To what degree is each initiative actually implemented?" and "If the initiative is implemented, what is the impact on student achievement and other organizational goals?" For example, we have observed a school system purchase online curriculum resources with the assumption that teachers would use the program to link standards, curriculum, assessment, and teaching. But when we simply asked, "Is anyone really using this?" we found fewer than 1 percent of teachers had even accessed the program. This is not an isolated example, as schools are inundated with programs for data analysis, formative assessment, and literacy interventions that are delivered but never or rarely used (Reeves, 2006). Leaders should be assessing the degree to which a particular initiative is having the desired impact. Simply asking the question about degree of implementation will reveal the *binary fallacy*—that is, the assumption that an initiative is either implemented or not implemented. But human performance is almost never binary, but rather takes place on a continuum. On one end of that continuum is delivery—teachers attend a workshop, receive workbooks, and perhaps log instructions for a technology-based tool. The second level of implementation goes beyond delivery, but includes actual evidence that teachers are using the initiative. The third level includes not only the use of the initiative but also evidence that these new professional practices have a positive impact on student results. The fourth level includes not only student results but also evidence that successful implementation is replicated by other educators and leaders in the school. In other words, saying "We have the program" never tells a complete story of an initiative's implementation.

Step 3: Make a Not-to-Do List

Prior to embarking on new plans, leaders must establish a clear and emphatic not-to-do list. Before you set goals for the next one hundred days, identify in specific terms those tasks, projects, priorities, and initiatives that you will *not* do. Make the list public. Before you ask your staff to implement the 100-day plan, tell them what they can *stop* doing.

Step 4: Identify 100-Day Challenges

Identify your top-priority challenges for the next one hundred days. Be specific. They might relate to reducing student failure or improving discipline, parental engagement, attendance, or staff morale—you decide. But you must set specific and measurable goals with which you can make an impact in one hundred days.

Step 5: Monitor High-Leverage Practices

Identify specific professional practices that you will implement immediately. These need not be major changes, such as adopting a new curriculum or assessment system, but practices that you and the staff can apply immediately, such as the following.

- Effectively monitoring collaborative team meetings within the PLC
- Changing a schedule to allocate more instructional time to areas where data suggest students need more help
- Shifting staff meeting time to allow for collaborative scoring of student work
- Scheduling three common formative assessments in the next one hundred days

In other words, select short-term, achievable goals whose implementation you can clearly observe.

Step 6: Specify Results

Finally, identify the results that you will measure. Consider how to display these results in an easily understandable visual featuring before-and-after data. Examples of results include the following.

- Reading comprehension
- Writing proficiency
- Mathematics proficiency
- Attendance
- Parental engagement
- Consistency of scoring
- Student engagement

The six steps are a process of identification, measurement, delegation, and elimination that makes way for aligning focus on the greatest priorities of the system.

Part 1 closes with a description of the six steps in action. The appendix contains a template to aid in creating your 100-day plan (see page 126).

Part 2: Creating the Environment for Success

In part 2, we consider the environment for success for 100-day leaders and the educational systems they guide. The primary organizing structure for effective educational systems is the PLC. Consisting of collaborative teams that focus on core questions for student results, PLCs allow all people within the system—teachers, paraprofessionals, students, parents, leaders, and community members—to understand how they can personally support the system's goals. The Collaborative Team Rubric in the appendix (see page 128) provides scales for use in assessing PLC practice within teams.

Putting It All Together

We conclude this book with a focus on accountability and resilience. There are times when leaders must, in our vernacular, "put their stars on the table." That expression stems from the occasions in which military generals must honor their principles and values above the political demands of the moment. By relinquishing their stars, they express a willingness to lose their authority, position, and professional security in order to establish the primacy of integrity over obedience. We believe that the heavy emphasis on test-based accountability in the first two decades of the 21st century has amounted to an exercise in frustration. While student scores are certainly important, those scores tell only a fraction of the story of teachers', administrators', and students' hard work. Our view of *accountability*, framed by the work of Richard DuFour, Douglas

Reeves, and Rebecca DuFour (2018), is holistic and includes not only what students produce in terms of literacy, mathematics, and other scores but also what causes those scores. We therefore consider the *accountability variables* that teachers and leaders can control—the measurable and specific actions in the classroom, school, and district that lead to the results teachers and leaders seek to achieve.

Resilience refers to how 100-day leaders persevere in the face of overwhelming obstacles. Some change literature has claimed that systemic change occurs only after five to seven years (Fullan, 2018; Kotter, 1996). Imagine that you are the parent of a kindergarten student and you hear that effective change in literacy instruction will happen when your child enters middle school. An anonymous friend of ours has said that school change happens "one funeral at a time." We are unwilling to accept this cynical view, and therefore claim that history and experience show that change can happen much faster—in one hundred days.

If you don't believe us, believe Abraham Lincoln and Franklin D. Roosevelt. As you shall see, educational leaders around the world have proven that 100-day leaders can make a remarkable and enduring difference in a very short time.

PART 1

EXPLORING
100-DAY LEADERSHIP

CHAPTER 1

WHY BEFORE HOW: THE MORAL IMPERATIVE OF LEADERSHIP

ABRAHAM LINCOLN IS credited with saving the Union and emancipating the slaves. But as any student of history knows, achieving these goals came at an enormous cost in blood and treasure, and success was not at all certain during the dark days of the early 1860s. Although the Emancipation Proclamation is, in retrospect, regarded as a great victory for the advancement of equality and the pursuit of the Declaration of Independence's noble goal that "all men are created equal," even the Northern states did not have consensus on this when the Proclamation was announced. Lincoln faced opposition in his cabinet, in Congress, among many governors in states that had not joined the Confederacy, and, most notably, among the generals leading the Union army.

Presidential scholar and historian Doris Kearns Goodwin (2018) notes that before Ulysses S. Grant secured the surrender of Robert E. Lee at Appomattox Court House, the Union suffered a series of disastrous military leaders, including George McClellan, who regarded emancipation as an abomination and who warned that Northern troops would desert in droves if slavery were abolished. These soldiers, he claimed, fought for the Union, not for the enslaved. McClellan's failure to pursue Southern armies more vigorously, Goodwin (2018) notes, nearly cost the Union the war. In brief, Lincoln did not wait for buy-in from politicians and generals, but followed the moral authority that he perceived as an unalterable course. He acted on not what was popular but what was right and just. In his address to Congress on the issue, he said:

> Fellow-citizens, we cannot escape history. . . . The fiery trial through which we pass, will light us down, in honor or dishonor, to the latest generation. . . . In *giving* freedom to the *slave*, we *assure* freedom to the *free*—honorable alike in what we give and what we preserve. We shall nobly save, or meanly lose, the last best hope of earth. (Goodwin, 2018, pp. 241–242)

Goodwin (2018) concludes, "It was through the language of his leadership that a moral purpose and meaning was imprinted upon the protracted misery of the Civil War" (p. 242). Lincoln exercised transformational leadership at its best—leadership in pursuit of a moral purpose, not political gain or popularity (Goodwin, 2018).

Moral Authority in Education

In education, leadership based on moral authority is the key to sustaining educational results and organizational health. The title and administrative authority of a leadership role pales in comparison with moral authority, which no title can bestow. Titles are designated; moral authority is earned. This requires leaders who have the will and the courage to lead—to act, and then to persist in the face of adversity and opposition. Whether the leader is a veteran or new to the position, every few months bring new opportunities for beginnings. Every day people get to choose. Hopefully, they will choose to focus on the ultimate moral purpose of schooling—enhancing student learning. The most complex and challenging multiyear objectives, such as building systemwide capacity for technology integration, planning and executing building projects, or overhauling special education services, all begin with moral purpose. Access to technology is an equity issue, bridging the opportunity gap between rich and poor. Planning and executing building projects is not about bricks and mortar, but about providing access and equity for students and creating the most effective educational environment for all students. Architects, masons, welders, bricklayers, plumbers, and carpenters all engage in a school building project with a moral purpose at their core. They are not merely assembling a building, they are creating a learning environment. All of their efforts, ultimately, will have a direct or indirect impact on the quality of education that occurs within a district or school. Their moral purpose today is similar to the craftsmen of medieval times when they were not merely laying bricks, but building a cathedral. Improving special education delivery, whether it involves extending services to students who need them or removing the *special education* label from wrongly identified students, is an equity issue as well.

A fantasy view of leadership supposes that as long as you have just cause and clear evidence, change will happen naturally, like how children learn to speak or crawl. But organizational change does not happen that way. Leaders must establish the momentum and critical groundwork for success for any initiative in the first one hundred days. It is unreasonable to think that significant cultural change will simply bubble up from the bottom if the leader just gets out of the way and allows it to happen. Effective change is not an all-or-nothing affair in which the leader must lead either domineeringly or submissively. Ironically, meaningful bottom-up leadership requires exceptional top-down leadership in order to flourish (DuFour et al., 2016).

Essential Elements of Leadership

What leaders aspire to do often differs greatly from what they actually accomplish. The question, then, is, What leadership behaviors have links to improved results? A synthesis of the best research on the relationship between leadership and student achievement (Reeves, 2016b) reveals seven essential elements of leadership.

1. Purpose
2. Trust
3. Focus
4. Leverage
5. Feedback
6. Change
7. Sustainability

Consider the evidence behind each of these elements.

Purpose

Ordinary leaders might ask a colleague, "What do you do?" or "What is your job?" Extraordinary leaders instead ask, "What are you passionate about?" Real purpose stems not from a job requirement, but from passion. An excellent way to use a staff meeting is to ask your colleagues to complete the following sentence frame: "Because I passionately believe _____, I am committed to _____." For example, a teacher may say, "Because I passionately believe that all students deserve the opportunity to succeed, I am committed to ensuring that every student receives personal encouragement, feedback, and support every day." The leader does not simply launch into a workshop on formative assessment or effective feedback practices, but rather first taps into the passionate beliefs of the faculty.

A survey of teachers reveals that teachers are far less likely to change their practices due to administrative requirements than due to evidence and collegial interaction (*Education Week*, 2018). According to this survey, twice as many teachers receive their ideas from conferences and interactions with colleagues as teachers who receive their ideas from social media—a margin of 78 percent to 40 percent (*Education Week*, 2018). And how do teachers turn ideas into practice? Three times as many teachers say that evidence is their primary motivator as teachers who receive their primary motivation from endorsements from their administrators—a margin of 39 percent to 13 percent (*Education Week*, 2018). This strongly suggests that administrative commands will not influence teaching and learning as much as compelling cases that leaders make with evidence and passion.

Some leaders think that they will create a sense of purpose with their mission and vision statements. Rick DuFour used to joke that he could create a mission statement generator that would automatically produce what committees come up with after pondering and laboring for hours with the help of a strategic planning consultant. It would come up with something like this:

> Our mission is to create productive citizens of the 21st century who will excel in creativity, critical thinking, communication, and every other alliterative word or phrase that we can think of as they prepare for a multicultural world, ready to face the challenges, blah, blah, blah, while valuing the unique contributions and skills of every stakeholder irrespective of differences in learning style or preference, and enhancing the blah, blah, blah.

You get the idea. The only people who remember mission statements like this, if only for a few days, are the people who wrote them.

Contrast the ponderous and useless mission statements that are so prevalent in schools with that of the Advent School (n.d.) in Boston: "Learn with passion, act with courage, and change the world." A seven-year-old at this school could explain what the statement means.

- **How do students learn with passion?** "I go to the library anytime I want, not just when it's library time!"
- **How do students act with courage?** "My friend has dyslexia, but she's really smart. When the teacher gave her an easy book, I said, 'She's not stupid—she just doesn't

read very fast—and she should be reading the same hard
books that I get.'"

- **How do students change the world?** "We collect canned
goods for the homeless shelter, and we pick up trash on
the street. We even came up with some ideas about how to
not pollute water and how to make the playground safer."

We're not suggesting that this is the right mission statement for
your school, but this experience does suggest a couple of acid-test
questions. First, can a seven-year-old explain what your mission
statement means? Second, does the mission statement resonate with
everyone in the school who can use it as a springboard for guiding
daily actions?

Trust

In their landmark leadership study, James M. Kouzes and Barry
Z. Posner (2011) identify *credibility* as the most important attribute
for leadership success. Staff will forgive leaders for their mistakes in
data analysis, communication, charisma, and myriad other leadership requirements as long as staff trust them. But if leaders lose credibility, it doesn't matter how competent they are in other fields. Data
analysis and charisma mean nothing without credibility. Credible
leaders do what they say they will do. Therefore, within the first one
hundred days of taking a leadership role, we recommend a rhythm
of "promises made, promises kept" for every meeting: "Last week,
I promised that I would do this, and here is how I have kept that
promise." Credible leaders should make this phrase the hallmark of
every single encounter with their staff. This commitment to promises made, promises kept is an obligation of not merely the leader,
but the entire system. It creates reciprocal accountability in which
the leader makes and keeps promises and the staff do the same. Here
are some examples of promises made, promises kept.

- "At our last meeting, we agreed to bring student work for collaborative scoring to our team meetings, and this week, we have that work and are ready to go."
- "At our last meeting, we agreed to bring a list of individual students who need intervention and specific strategies to help them succeed, and this week, we have that list right here."

In the ideal world we advocate, every board meeting, cabinet meeting, department meeting, grade-level meeting, and collaborative team meeting has the same rhythm of promises made, promises kept.

Focus

We can all agree that the amount of incoming information educational leaders, teachers, students, and society at large have exposure to has expanded markedly since the early 1980s. Yet it's safe to say that the amount of learning has not markedly increased. Where does all of this transmitted but unused information go? It is lost to *fragmentation*, the inevitable result of futile attempts to multitask and absorb information at an increasingly frantic pace. Fragmentation, not focus, is the norm in the 21st century. Our research suggests, however, that *focus*—the prioritization of no more than six initiatives for any school or system—is strongly related to gains in student learning (Reeves, 2011b). Unfortunately, focus is elusive. Fragmentation does not occur due to malice on anyone's part; it stems from noble motives. Have lots of high-poverty students? Here's a new program! Have lots of English learners? Here's another new program! Have lots of special education students? Here's another new initiative! But however noble the motivations, fragmentation is associated with significantly lower levels of student learning. Indeed, schools with high concentrations of students from low-income families, students learning English, and special education students are the least likely to have high levels of focus (Reeves, 2011b). In our studies of more than two thousand schools, those with six or fewer initiatives have the greatest gains in student achievement (Reeves, 2011b).

We are aware that the danger of focus is *FOMO*—fear of missing out. If a neighboring district has a new initiative and you don't, then you think that you might fall behind. This logic undermines deep implementation of initiatives. We have seen this many times in schools as they journey to become PLCs.

Leverage

Archimedes (n.d.) said, "Give me a place to stand on and with a lever I will move the whole world." He was right, as any high school physics student can tell you. It would require a very, very long lever to move the mass of the earth (though probably not any longer than the lever required to move schools and classrooms). Educational leaders face a bewildering array of strategies that claim to work— that is, practices that influence student achievement. But this "What works?" approach to making choices is ultimately futile because, as John Hattie (2009) has joked, anything with a pulse *works*. The more insightful question to ask is, "What works best; what has the most leverage?" Leaders need to make the distinction between the much-vaunted standard of *statistical significance* and the more important standard of *practical significance*, or what in medicine is called *clinical significance*. Although marketing literature overflows with claims of statistical significance, usually followed by multiple exclamation points, statistical significance is actually a very low bar. A difference in student achievement of only a few percentage points may be statistically significant—that is, the difference between the control group and the experimental group is unlikely due to random variation. In general, the larger the sample size, the easier it is to establish statistical significance, even if that difference is very small.

The more relevant question for educational leaders and teachers to ask is: "Does this proposal have practical significance—does it have so great an impact that we should stop doing other things in order to start doing this new initiative?" Most educational systems adopt initiatives one on top of another—the additive mode. But the principle of leverage suggests that you can't move the earth while you are also attempting to move every other planet. In order to move the educational planet, leaders must stop attempting to move everything else in the solar system and focus on those elements of leverage that have the greatest potential for student gains.

So, what are the leverage points in education? Our research suggests three central points of leverage. The first leverage point is the comprehensive use of PLCs as the central organizing principle for every school. In a review of 196 schools including more than a quarter million students (Reeves, 2016b), we find that when schools implement PLCs at Work® with depth and duration, significant student achievement gains in reading, mathematics, and science occur. The longer the implementation, the greater the gains. This clearly distinguishes the schools that go to a conference, gain superficial buy-in, declare victory, and move on from those that have long-term commitments to PLCs. The greatest gains happen in those schools that, year after year, maintain a laser-like focus on successful and deep PLC implementation. With each additional year after initial implementation, achievement gains grow, from three to five to seven to ten years (Reeves, 2010). This dogged persistence and focus prevents schools from yielding to the siren call of the latest fad and helps them remain committed to the collaborative processes that matter most for student results.

Feedback

Feedback is the second leverage point. Of all the tools that teachers and leaders have available to influence student achievement, effective feedback has some of the greatest impact on student results. No matter how good the curriculum, data analysis, projects, or other elements of instruction that schools use, all of these have little value without effective feedback. Indeed, we have argued that many tests masquerading as formative assessments are better described as *uninformative assessments* (Reeves, 2011b). Even the most sophisticated assessments are useless unless teachers use the results to inform teaching and learning. The most elegant curriculum is valueless if educators merely deliver it and do not accompany it with effective feedback on the degree to which students are learning it.

The acronym *FAST* summarizes the four elements of effective feedback: (1) fair, (2) accurate, (3) specific, and (4) timely (Reeves, 2016a). You can identify feedback you have received—from, say, a great coach or music director—that energized or encouraged you. Similarly, you can think of times when you received demoralizing and inconsequential feedback. Imagine that during your anniversary dinner, your spouse announces, "Honey, it's time for your annual performance review. Here are some areas where you have exceeded my expectations, and here are some developmental opportunities." If that example makes you cringe, then so should the vast majority of educational feedback systems, which provide vague, inconsistent information to students, teachers, and leaders, and deliver it long after anyone can do anything about it.

The greatest potential for leaders to improve feedback and achieve great short-term, 100-day goals lies in two areas: (1) how leaders provide feedback to teachers and (2) how teachers provide feedback to students. Most teacher evaluation systems are the opposite of FAST; they are unfair (different administrators evaluate the same performance differently), they are inaccurate (observation rubrics are ambiguous and student learning scores are widely inaccurate), they are ambiguous (teachers do not routinely get specific feedback to improve performance), and they are late (end-of-year observations are toxic and demoralizing).

Similarly, the way that teachers grade students' work violates every element of the FAST framework. Fairness is all about consistency, and our research reveals that the same student could receive grades of A, B, C, D, or F for identical performance, based on differences in teachers' idiosyncratic grading systems (Reeves, 2015). Grades are notoriously inaccurate because the grade may reflect not the student's proficiency in the subject being graded, but a host of other factors, ranging from parental support to literacy. Grades are rarely specific, as four students could receive a grade of C for entirely different reasons, such as proficiency, attitude, participation, and parental advocacy. And grades are rarely timely—the first sign of trouble is a low mark at the end of the semester when, in fact, schools know within the first two weeks of the semester whether students are in danger of failure. We have seen schools that have elaborate and sophisticated data warehouses and the information they need to identify and intervene for students who are at grave risk of failure, but they fail to transform this information into decisive leadership actions. It is as if the students are patients who submit to an expensive and detailed diagnostic procedure that yields important information for life-saving treatment but the hospital sends them home without a treatment plan or a word from the physician.

In sum, even though leaders know that feedback is a critical ingredient of success, they often squander this essential resource, and the feedback to teachers and students fails to meet the essential requirements of effectiveness.

The third leverage point is nonfiction writing. When students write to describe, compare, evaluate, or persuade, they engage their critical-thinking faculties and build literacy skills. Our research concludes that nonfiction writing is associated not only with improved composition skills but also with improvements in reading comprehension, mathematics, science, and social studies (Reeves, 2002). Our research in successful high-poverty schools reveals the profound impact of nonfiction writing. In low-performing schools, the vast majority of student writing was fiction, fantasy, poetry, or personal narrative. In high-performing schools with similar demographic characteristics, there was a much more balanced approach in student writing, including expository, persuasive, and descriptive writing (Reeves, in press).

Change

Our friend Michael Fullan is an international authority on change leadership. He is often associated with the claim that systemic change requires five to seven years. But over dinner one night, Michael said, "I've learned a few things about change in the thirty-five years since I originally wrote about the long-term nature of change, and that includes how to accelerate the pace of change" (M. Fullan, personal communication, December 4, 2016). The central argument of this book is that meaningful change can take place in one hundred days, and that if leaders fail to achieve short-term wins, they will never have the momentum necessary for long-term success. Why is change leadership so important? Because schools are dynamic systems, facing new and complex challenges every year. Administrators who fail to engage in effective change leadership will preside over an organization that is doomed to regression and stagnation.

Sustainability

The enduring finding of the research on effective educational change is that *practices, not programs* have the greatest impact on change (Reeves, 2011b). We are strong advocates of PLCs, but we frame our advocacy with the conviction that these collaborative practices become part of school culture—*the way we do things around here*—and not a transient initiative.

Summary

In this chapter, we suggest that leadership is a moral imperative and introduce the six-step framework for how to transform those ideals into action. People won't care about the *how* of change until they embrace the *why*—the moral imperative that frames their obligations to stakeholders and that sets the context for their daily commitments. Long-term plans have no meaning unless leaders contextualize them with clear short-term actions and results. In order to achieve this, leaders must master the essential elements of effective leadership: purpose, trust, focus, leverage, feedback, change, and sustainability. In the next chapter, we examine the six steps of 100-day leadership plans in more detail.

CHAPTER 2

THE SIX STEPS OF 100-DAY LEADERSHIP

ONE-HUNDRED-DAY LEADERSHIP IS a continuous process. Too many strategic and school-improvement plans lend themselves only to review at the end of the school year or at the conclusion of the three- to five-year time structure of the plan. By contrast, the 100-day leader is engaged in monitoring progress every day and making midcourse corrections at least every one hundred days. Leaders achieve this continuous process through the following six steps.

1. Identify your values.
2. Take an initiative inventory.
3. Make a not-to-do list.
4. Identify 100-day challenges.
5. Monitor high-leverage practices.
6. Specify results.

In this chapter, we explore each of these steps.

Step 1: Identify Your Values

Educational leaders are often the architects of compromise, considering a variety of divergent views and skillfully blending them into policies and practices that are acceptable to the vast majority of staff members. However, there are two areas where compromise is not appropriate—safety and values. If there is not a safe environment for students and staff, then learning is nearly impossible. Safety is not a matter of opinion, but rather an essential requirement for the entire learning community. Similarly, core values are not a matter of personal opinion, to be accepted or rejected as a result of personal taste, but rather are the bedrock principles on which a school operates. Consider this: Stanley Sanders, a fictional character who is a composite of many leaders we have encountered, was known as a taciturn, collaborative leader who respected and protected his teachers, and had a remarkable ability to listen and build consensus among his faculty; he had perfected the *look*—the countenance that conveyed to everyone that the discussion was over. Mr. Sanders's line of demarcation was safety and values. He would listen, some said endlessly, to debate and discussion about pedagogy, research, motivation, and technique. But when the topic of discussion turned into the realm of safety and values, his friendly eyes turned to steel, and his solicitous demeanor became dictatorial. It was the look, and everyone knew the words that would follow: "Colleagues, this is a safety issue, so there are no shades of gray." He would add with a slight grin, "I'm not asking for a show of hands on this."

He applied the look judiciously but consistently. Months could pass without any hint of administrative authority, but then would come the day, for example, when a new teacher would say that she'd had a professor who didn't believe in phonics instruction for teaching reading. "Ms. Moore," he said in his courteous but deliberate tone, "reading instruction in this school is a safety issue. It's as important as crosswalk safety, cafeteria hygiene, and fire drills, and we don't vote on fire drills."

This took Ms. Moore, a dedicated and earnest educator, aback. She joined the faculty of McEachern Elementary School because she had heard that the principal was committed to consensus and that teachers had a voice in the operation of the school. Her favorite college professor wore a lapel pin featuring the word *phonics* with a red line through it. He was a star—presenting at the International Literacy Association conference and well published in his field. His students adored him and adopted his belief that students learn to read naturally, just as they learn to speak and crawl. "Just put the books in the hands of children," he said.

Mr. Sanders's view of reading instruction—a core skill for every elementary school principal—seemed old-fashioned. But in this encounter, Mr. Sanders presented 21st century evidence that was overwhelming. It showed that students learn to read through receiving direct instruction, learning letter sounds and consonant blends, having consistent exposure to fun and interesting books, and reading orally and silently. "Sorry, Ms. Moore," said Mr. Sanders. "This is a safety issue—when children don't learn to read, they are at risk for multiple failures in future years, and that means eventual failure in high school. Students who fail in high school are much more likely to have serious medical conditions and are much more likely to be involved in the criminal justice system. So, reading—and the effective teaching of reading—is a safety issue. We protect our students from safety risks like fires and traffic in crosswalks, and we're going to protect them from ineffective reading instruction."

Then Mr. Sanders turned to the school's values, which the faculty accepted year after year. They seemed prosaic to Ms. Moore—the sort of values one might see on any school's list.

- **Respect:** "We treat people as we would like to be treated."
- **Kindness:** "We care about the feelings of others."
- **Integrity:** "We tell the truth, even when it's not easy."
- **Excellence:** "Every student and adult strives to be the best he or she can be."
- **Reason:** "We teach and learn based on evidence, not popular beliefs, integrity, and excellence."

The first four were familiar to her—the stuff of corny framed posters that hang in the offices of principals around the world. But *reason*—she had not seen that one before. How could reason appear in the same list as kindness and respect?

The answer, Mr. Sanders explained every year, was that educators needed to have an agreed-on body of knowledge that guided their practices, like physicians, attorneys, or engineers do. If engineers followed personal philosophies rather than the laws of physics, buildings would collapse. If physicians followed folklore rather than science, patients would die. And if teachers followed politically influenced philosophies rather than scientific research, students would not learn to read. Reason—evidence-based practice—was as important to Mr. Sanders as kindness and respect.

The 100-day leader must establish values that are worth fighting for.

Values and the 100-Day Leader

Values, when well created, establish not only what an organization will do but also what it will not do. For example, many schools and educational systems have the value of respect, and if they take that value seriously, they would confront any violation of that value and say, "You disrespected a colleague, and that's a violation of our values!" But the truth is that value statements are one thing; values in action are quite another. If the school has the value of respect, and the leader notices a person grandstanding, pontificating, or ignoring the statements of a colleague in a faculty meeting, then the leader has the obligation to say, "Let's take a time-out. We have a value of respect, and it's my obligation to ensure that we honor our values. Mary just made a really important point, and some people were texting under the table, others were reading emails, and others were grading papers. Friends, that's disrespectful and a violation of our core value of respect. I'd like to do a reset, and ask Mary to start over, with all of us focusing on what she has to say and honoring our value of respect."

Note well that a focus on values is not angry, dominating, or overwhelming. It just compares the group's behavior with its values. When a group truly institutionalizes its values, the leader will not hold responsibility for noting every conflict between values and current reality; every group member will say, or signal, that the behavior at hand is not consistent with values.

Values Worth Fighting For

We recommend the *law of parsimony* in selecting values. That is, simple and clear explanations are more useful than those that are unnecessarily complex and convoluted. For example, many long-winded honor codes and policy statements for academic dishonesty could be replaced by the simple statement, "We do not lie, cheat, or steal or tolerate those who do." Another example, many Eastern and Western religious traditions have variations on the same theme: love your neighbor as yourself. When the Dalai Lama and Archbishop Desmond Tutu (2016) met, they found much more in common than the traditions and religious differences that might have separated them. When it comes to creating values, 100-day leaders might find the example of these two spiritual leaders useful. Separated by continents, cultures, beliefs, and traditions, they nevertheless found common ground. And 100-day leaders can do the same. We cannot tell you what your values should be, as these will reflect your deepest sense of who you are as a person and as a leader. But we can say this: leaders who are not crystal clear about their values and who fail to communicate those values clearly and consistently through words and actions will not earn the trust of their colleagues.

Step 1 ensures that 100-day leaders live by their values. These statements of bone-deep belief do not need to have the eloquence of Demosthenes but do require the simple moral imperative of the language of Lincoln. There is a difference between proposals, which are debatable, and values, which are not. As Mr. Sanders says, "We don't vote on fire drills." If it's a matter of safety or values, then the decision has already been made. We are not arguing that you should adopt a particular set of values—we leave that for you, the reader, to decide. But it is absolutely essential that values match actions. If, for example, leaders have the value of reason, then they must embrace evidence-based practices and reject those that are more associated with politics and personal philosophy. If leaders have the value of respect, then they must not tolerate—and they must publicly challenge—disrespectful behavior.

We now turn our attention to the second step of the 100-day leader: take an initiative inventory, or, as we also call it, *clear the decks.* We have witnessed many well-intentioned leaders who knew the right things to do but could never get started because they were unable or unwilling to deal with the things *not* to do. They were all over best practices, but they could not identify and weed out worst practices. We now approach the most challenging leadership decision: "weeding the garden in order to plant the flowers."

Step 2: Take an Initiative Inventory

We have a dear friend, let's call him Dr. B, who is one of the best educational leaders we have encountered. He is beloved by his staff, board, and community. When we asked Dr. B for a list of his district's instructional initiatives, he replied emphatically. "We believe in focus and prioritization," he said, and listed five thoughtful priorities. "Yes, sir," we responded, "but would it be OK if we asked your teachers?" In a simple email survey, we asked teachers to identify the instructional initiatives that they were responsible for implementing. In response to that inquiry, we discovered sixty-two different initiatives.

We never doubted Dr. B's sincerity, but there is a striking difference between the leader's intent and the classroom's daily reality. It was not that Dr. B failed to establish a focused agenda; rather, he failed to explicitly take initiatives off the table at the classroom level. Teachers certainly understood Dr. B's priorities, but they also had the priorities of his predecessor, and his predecessor's predecessor, and so on. Moreover, some teachers—thoughtful and great professionals all—still had the notebooks filled with curriculum and lessons they developed in their teacher preparation programs. Indeed, those bulging notebooks impressed the principals who first hired them, but, over time, no one had ever removed anything from their task lists; they simply added to them.

Our research and observation of schools has revealed that this challenge of keeping focus is particularly acute in schools that have high numbers of students in poverty, students learning English, and students with special needs. The higher the concentration of students with these challenges, the less likely the faculty focus on only a few initiatives. As needs grow, grants, requirements, and initiatives proliferate—all borne of good intentions. But when all these good intentions accumulate, no single initiative ever gets the time, attention, and deep implementation required to effectively impact student achievement. This leads to the *law of initiative fatigue* (Reeves, 2011b). This law says that however well intentioned the initiatives may be, once schools have more than six priorities, the impact on student achievement diminishes.

Although initiative fatigue is pervasive in schools, there is an answer to this challenge. The antidote for initiative fatigue lies in leaders utilizing a three-step initiative-analysis process. First and most importantly, schools and systems must take an initiative inventory. Second, they must create implementation rubrics for each initiative. Third, they must apply the rubrics at every school—class by class. These steps are collaborative processes, requiring the cooperation of every teacher and administrator.

Taking the Initiative Inventory

Schools must first count and label every instructional and leadership initiative. In our experience, this list is always longer than the senior leadership team thinks it is. We have found schools that have seven separate literacy programs, all competing for time within the same literacy block, and none of which implemented as intended. We have found teachers consumed with varying data-analysis programs, losing precious team time entering data into notebooks, exercising compliance rather than analysis. And while overwhelming evidence shows that PLCs, implemented deeply and well, are key to improving teaching and learning, we grieve that some schools schedule what they call *PLC time*, rather than deeply implementing the process, that never addresses the core issues of learning, assessment, intervention, and enrichment.

The essence of effective 100-day leadership is focus, and that will never happen without an honest assessment of the burdens on teachers and administrators. Taking the initiative inventory is not just the work of teachers and building principals. We have found that initiative fatigue also afflicts central office departments. There are overwhelming demands in special education, human resources, technology, and every other department. To have an impact, 100-day leaders must first identify every single initiative the school has in place.

Creating Implementation Rubrics

The second step of the initiative-analysis process is the creation of implementation rubrics for each initiative. Although we recommend the use of very specific rubrics, here is a general outline of what the four-point implementation rubrics might look like.

- **Level 1:** We have the materials, but we have not yet begun implementation.
- **Level 2:** We have trained the staff, but there is minimal implementation by only a few early adopters.
- **Level 3:** We have achieved full implementation by more than 90 percent of the staff.
- **Level 4:** We have achieved full implementation and have clear evidence of the effect on student results.

We have found that many faculties get stuck in level 2. They have the materials and they have the training, but well before teachers have the opportunity to begin effective implementation and potentially progress to level 3, other initiatives come along, with new materials, new workshops, and new priorities. This creates the chronic state of initiative fatigue. There is clearly a big jump between level 2 and level 3, which contributes to a lack of deep implementation. As daunting as the prospect of 90 percent of teachers implementing an initiative may seem, it is important to note that the goal is not 100 percent. We have seen too many leaders squander energy and time trying to get the last 1 or 2 percent of teachers to accept an initiative when that time and energy would be better spent nurturing and encouraging the 90 percent of teachers who are doing everything that the leader has asked and more.

In a surprising research finding, we learned that the relationship between the depth of implementation of initiatives and the impact on student results is not linear (Reeves, 2006). We had hypothesized that with greater implementation—in other words, as a school progressed from level 1 to level 2, to level 3, to level 4—student achievement would improve. We were dead wrong. In fact, the impact on student achievement changed very little from level 1 to level 2 to level 3. Middling efforts are no better than low-level implementation. Only at level 4, the highest level of implementation, does implementation have a significant impact on student results. In other words, as Bob Eaker might say, "If you're not going to go whole hog, then don't bother."

Applying the Rubrics

The third step of the initiative analysis is to apply the rubrics at every school—class by class. This usually requires some combination of interviews, surveys, direct observations, and focus groups. The reason for this inquiry is to distinguish between the appearance of implementation—the presence of materials and participation in workshops—and the actual implementation of initiatives. For example, we have observed many schools that claim to have "PLC time" have invested in materials, workshops, and institutes to learn about PLCs. But when we ask about some of the essential elements of PLCs, such as common formative assessments or evidence that teachers are addressing the central questions of learning, assessment, intervention, and extension, we find that "PLC time" is just another label for a faculty meeting. Rather than explicit intervention and enrichment plans based on recent student assessment, the conversation is dominated by discussions of discipline, parental engagement, and individual plans for lessons. Thus we do not ask, "Are you doing PLCs?" but rather systematically inquire about the practices associated with deep implementation of PLCs. We have limited confidence in most surveys; teachers might say, "Sure, we're implementing writer's workshop," but direct observation might reveal little in the way of peer editing, multiple drafts, and conferences—the very core of an effective writer's workshop. If leaders want to learn the degree of implementation of this initiative, then they need to personally look at writing portfolios for evidence of improved writing that results from editing, rewriting, and following the writer's workshop process.

Assessing the degree of initiative implementation does not come without pain. We have learned the hard way that when a leader identifies an expensive initiative that has not been effectively implemented and hence has no impact on student results, staff members do not hail the leader as a conquering hero. Rather than saying, "Thanks for saving us $100,000 on an initiative we were not using," some staff members will more likely respond, "But we need that program!" Every turkey has a champion—somebody who will defend a demonstrably ineffective and unused initiative, because he or she authorized the purchase in the first place. This process requires courage, an essential attribute of the 100-day leader.

In this section, we considered the reality of the law of initiative fatigue and described a three-step process for defeating it. This requires taking an initiative inventory and then creating four-point rubrics for the implementation of each initiative. Finally, this process requires assessing the actual implementation of each initiative at every school. Although this process is unpopular, it is essential. Leaders cannot focus on priorities when they have too many of them. They must say no to some popular ideas that, however promising when adopted, have no chance of influencing student achievement. We now move on to the next step to becoming a 100-day leader, make a not-to-do list.

Step 3: Make a Not-to-Do List

Everyone has a *to-do list*—the never-ending list of tasks and projects to be done. Only rarely do we see leaders who have created an explicit *not-to-do list*—that is, the tasks and projects that they will deliberately remove from their list and then delegate or discard. Whenever we challenge leaders to make a not-to-do list, the most frequent response is, "There's nothing I can take off my list. Everything is mandatory and everything is important!" The truth is that everyone has a not-to-do list—it's just an unconscious list.

When the end of the year arrives, there are many tasks and projects that were never finished. These items, by default, wound up on the unconscious not-to-do list. We argue that leaders are much better served by a conscious list of tasks that they will stop doing. We have conducted a not-to-do challenge in many of our leadership seminars. "If you are to apply any of the learnings of today," we say respectfully, "you will need to stop doing something that is now occupying your time and attention. What will you stop doing?" The most consistent response we receive is silence. We wish to respectfully push back. Here are some ideas you might consider for your not-to-do list related to email and other communication, meetings, and ineffective practice.

Email and Other Communication

Many leaders devote more than two hours a day to responding to email (Newport, 2016). We believe it is actually more than that because the two hours are not concentrated in a single block but rather distributed throughout the day. Every time an alert sounds for an incoming email, it distracts the leader and, thinking that he or she is providing great service, he or she stops and responds to one, and another, and then another. This demonstrates the myth of multitasking, which is, in fact, *switch-tasking*. When leaders switch tasks in this way, an entire day can evaporate without completion of a single substantive task (Crenshaw, 2008). This is the reason, we are convinced, that we receive emails from educational leaders with time stamps after ten in the evening and before six in the morning; they cannot sustain such a pace.

Conquering the email beast is difficult, but possible. We know of very successful educational leaders who have simply unplugged from email. We realize this is a radical idea, but consider this: What if the administrative assistant gets every email and prioritizes the very few of those that require leadership attention, and then the leader answers just those few? If that solution seems too extreme, consider using the Manage Rules and Alerts email function (as the function is called in Microsoft Outlook) to narrow the focus of what you receive as the leader. For example, if someone copies you on an email instead of directly emailing you, the function puts the email in a different folder, and you ignore it. The idea is that if the message is not addressed to the leader, then it's not important for the leader to review. Leaders should also relentlessly identify and reject junk mail from vendors.

Leaders should take a similar approach to other forms of communication, like text messages and phone calls. Some of the most effective time managers we know have two different email addresses, text addresses, and phone numbers. One is the general address or number that everyone uses. The other is for priorities—family and leadership emergencies. For example, Superintendent Roger León of Newark Public Schools in Newark, New Jersey, gives every student in the district his general email address. They write messages such as, "Bro—we need AC in this classroom!" And to his enormous credit, Mr. León responds. But he keeps that email account separate, and he can allocate his time and attention to students when it is appropriate, and to leadership and personal priorities when that is appropriate. In sum, adding limiting email and other communications to the not-to-do list does not mean disrespecting stakeholders or disconnecting from the world, but instead focusing limited time on what matters most.

Meetings

In their masterful book *Time, Talent, Energy*, consultants Michael Mankins and Eric Garton (2017) assess the impact of meetings on what they call *organizational drag*. The authors explain that people find themselves wasting time on needless internal interactions, unproductive or inconsequential meetings, and unnecessary e-communications. They ask, provocatively, "Who in your organization has the authority to spend $15 million?" In most systems we have seen, that's the responsibility of a very senior person, even in the largest and most complex systems. But the truth is that the newest administrative assistant can spend that amount of money on a cycle of meetings that starts with senior leaders, and then cascades to additional meetings throughout the system. We have seen some leaders who put the cost of a meeting at the top of every agenda. For a typical school system cabinet with eight members earning an average of 100,000 dollars per year, that is 50 dollars per hour times eight people, or a minimum of 400 dollars per hour of meeting. If their cabinet meets weekly for two hours, that costs the district a minimum of 40,000 dollars per year (800 times 50 weeks). Do the same exercise for traditional faculty meetings and other administrator meetings and the cost is astronomical. The question leaders must address is whether these meetings are worth the cost. When they are dominated by announcements and presentations that do not require deliberation and discussion, then it quickly becomes apparent that most meetings are difficult to justify.

We have seen a coffee mug with the inscription, "I survived another meeting that could have been an email." We have observed an astonishing number of meetings that differ little from how a meeting would have gone in the early 20th century—oral announcements, endless information sharing, and posturing from one department to the next. The only purpose for a meeting, in our view, is deliberation and decision making. It is deeply ironic that schools expect teachers to have *flipped classrooms*—having students observe presentations at home, and then devoting classroom time to deliberation and discussion—yet cabinet meetings and leadership team meetings among administrators and teachers remain focused on a roundtable of presentations. It's OK to sing "Happy Birthday" in a staff meeting. But otherwise, voicing announcements is primitive. We have seen effective leaders conduct ten-minute stand-up meetings to focus on the most important issues, and then get back to work. We have seen senior leaders set quantitative goals to reduce the number of meetings and the number of person hours that they consume.

When we consider just the combination of ineffective meetings and unnecessary emails, the not-to-do list, which seemed so elusive earlier, soon becomes a very realistic goal.

Ineffective Practice

Thanks to scholars such as Anders Ericsson, educators know what effective practice looks like (Ericsson & Pool, 2017). *Gold standard practice*, as Ericsson calls it, requires coaching and feedback, differentiation, explicit goals, and the placement of students slightly outside their comfort zone (Ericsson & Pool, 2017). Yet an astonishing amount of practice in schools fails to meet these standards. Teachers assign homework because students need practice, yet homework consistently fails to meet gold standard practice. Moreover, homework has absolutely no impact on student performance (Neason, 2017). Worksheets in many classes require students to engage in sullen compliance rather than real learning, ensuring not that they master content, but that they loathe school. We know of principals who have limited access to the copy machine in order to stop the red tide of worksheets, but they are the exception. Teachers complain of never having enough time, yet they persist in assigning time-wasting worksheets that exhaust students and teachers alike.

Leaders no doubt have many more ways to save time than those we mention here in step 3, but if leaders could just address emails and other communications, meetings, and ineffective practices like worksheets, it would give them a great start to saving time as 100-day leaders.

Many leaders let trucks barrel through as students scramble for safety. But 100-day leaders stand their ground, protecting students, and protecting the leadership team tasked with safeguarding the interests of those students.

Now that the "decks are cleared" and there is time to focus on the essentials, we consider step 4, identify 100-day challenges.

Step 4: Identify 100-Day Challenges

In order to build credibility, 100-day leaders need some short-term wins. We have seen the following examples of 100-day challenges build credibility and confidence from the staff, students, and community. It's important to note that these examples come from real schools and districts, not composites or mythical systems. We know these people, and they achieve real results in one hundred days.

- Serrano Middle School, San Bernardino City Unified School District, San Bernardino, California: "We will reduce the eighth-grade D-F rate by more than two hundred students in an eight-hundred-student school."
- Mountain House High School, Lammersville Unified School District, Mountain House, California: "We will reduce our freshman and sophomore failure rate by more than 60 percent."
- Ben Davis High School, Metropolitan School District of Wayne Township, Indianapolis, Indiana: "We will reduce the ninth-grade science failure rate by 80 percent."
- Cardinal School District, Eldon, Iowa: "We will reduce the suspension rate by more than 50 percent."
- East Hartford Middle School, East Hartford School District, East Hartford, Connecticut: "We will reduce the truancy rate by 80 percent."

Although these schools and districts have differences in geography and demographic characteristics, they are consistent in their absolute commitment to student success. They illustrate the power of 100-day leadership—focused on short-term goals that lead to long-term results. And these schools are just the tip of the iceberg.

Although we do not presume to prescribe what 100-day results you should seek, our experience suggests that the goals should resonate with your community, teachers, and other stakeholders. Long-term goals, such as state and provincial test results, come too late. People need to know that their efforts are effective now with short-term goals in student performance, engagement, attendance, and behavior. They need clear comparisons, like the fall semester of this year compared with the fall semester of last year. For example, the goals might say the following.

- "Last year, 35 percent of students engaged in extracurricular activities. But we created a strong recruitment program for every club, sport, and activity, and this semester, we have 55 percent engagement. Our goal is to have 100 percent of students engaged in at least one activity."

- "Last year, 40 percent of our students read at grade level. This semester, it is slightly higher, at 48 percent, but we know that this is a critical need. So, we are implementing a schoolwide literacy support program, and next year, we will strive to have more than 60 percent of students reading at grade level. We will not rest until all our students achieve this goal."

- "Last year, we had thirty fights in our first one hundred days. We have studied our data, and we know where the fights happen, why they happen, and how we can prevent them. Our goal this year is zero fights in our first one hundred days."

- "We will build positive relationships with every student. In our first one hundred days, every teacher will know at least one thing about students outside of their academic performance, and we will place this into our student portfolios. We trust our teachers to find what is important for each student—a pet, a sport, a game, a sibling—but we will all know something about every student that has nothing to do with his or her grades or test scores."

Although 100-day leaders don't need a long list of goals, they do need to have a few things that will reveal the impact of their work in just one hundred days.

Because 100-day leaders concentrate on 100-day challenges, they have a remarkable degree of focus. When they wander the halls and visit classrooms, they know what they expect right now. They expect fewer fights, more students in classrooms, greater engagement in each class, consistent delivery of curriculum in every subject, and greater attention to detail in every collaborative team meeting. In step 4, leaders understand the results that they seek to achieve. Now we turn our attention to causes—the specific high-leverage practices that lead to those results.

Step 5: Monitor High-Leverage Practices

Most accountability systems focus only on effects—such as student test scores—not on causes, the measurable and observable actions of teachers and school leaders. By contrast, 100-day leaders focus on causes, not just effects. They know the high-leverage practices that have the strongest relationship to student achievement. For example, 100-day leaders know that deeper and more effective implementation of the PLC process is strongly associated with improved achievement in mathematics, English language arts, and science (Reeves, 2010). They know that deeper implementation of nonfiction writing is strongly associated with improved achievement in reading comprehension, mathematics, science, and social studies. They also know that focusing on results alone distorts their understanding of how to address the causes behind those results. We address high-leverage strategies and the results fallacy, and outline a 100-day learning system for monitoring high-leverage practices in this section.

High-Leverage Strategies

Teachers and educational leaders have limited time and extraordinary demands on the few free minutes that they have available. Therefore, they must look for *high-leverage strategies*—those few actions leaders and teachers can take that have the greatest impact on student results. This gives leaders an opportunity to distinguish between results that are *statistically* significant and those that are *clinically* significant. Imagine a salesperson enters your office and, with breathless enthusiasm, announces that he or she is offering a statistically significant program. But you, the 100-day leader, demur. You know that statistical significance is a pretty low bar—it just means in a peer-controlled environment, it unlikely will have relevance to your school; the control group and the experimental group had different results; and those differences were unlikely due to random variation. The 100-day leader demands more—not just statistical significance, but clinical significance. That is, the conclusive determination that if the leader implements one priority, such as PLC transformation or the strategy of nonfiction writing, then it is worth pulling the plug on other initiatives that, however popular, are no longer worth teachers' and leaders' time and attention.

The Results Fallacy

The *results fallacy* is the logical error that occurs when we confuse causes and effects. Focusing only on results distorts our understanding of how to address the causes of those results. For example, consider the obesity crisis. People are overweight at a higher rate than ever before, and this has dire consequences: diabetes, limb amputation, blindness. The consequences are so scary that many schools have decided to closely monitor the weight and the body mass index of every student. This result is predictable; the metric with the greatest public visibility—weight and body mass index— receives the most attention. But as a parent, wouldn't you want to know not just that your child is losing weight, but *how* your child is losing weight? You would want to know if the weight loss occurs as a result of an increase in healthy habits, such as a monitored diet and exercise, or as a result of dangerous means, such as an eating disorder or drug abuse. The result, in brief, does not tell the whole story. Similarly, 100-day leaders are wary of results alone, because they can only create a learning system if they also understand how those results are achieved.

The 100-Day Learning System

The most effective way to transform short-term efforts into long-term system-level learning is the 100-day learning system, what we have colloquially called the *science fair for schools*. For science fairs, students prepare a three-panel presentation using a standard format: the left panel states the challenge, the middle panel features the intervention (practice), and the right panel shows the results. Figure 2.1 shows an example. We have seen both leaders and teachers use this same format to effectively display their impact on student learning, behavior, parental engagement, attendance, and many other factors.

Challenge	Intervention	Results
Too many students are failing ninth-grade mathematics. Almost all failures are due to missing assignments and students giving up late in the semester.	Shift practice from homework to in-class practice. Change grading scale from 100 points to traditional A, B, C, D, F scale, with A = 4, B = 3, C = 2, D = 1, F = 0. Determine final grade based on student proficiency, not the average of grades during the semester.	The D-F rate improved from forty-four students the previous year to zero this year. Final exam scores increased, indicating higher levels of student learning and no grade inflation.

Source: Michael Doll, San Bernardino City Unified School District, San Bernardino California.

Figure 2.1: Three-panel presentation format for monitoring high-leverage practices.

Because teachers measure these changes within a single semester—no more than ninety days—they can make a clear-eyed comparison of student performance before and after the change in professional practices. Moreover, this practice overcomes the typical objection from many teachers and administrators to educational research who say "It's not relevant to our schools and our students." Of course, it is possible that the science fair approach will reveal ineffective professional practices—and we regard that as excellent news. This completely objective approach not only validates effective practices but also can invalidate fads and poor practices. Also, it simply invalidates the premise that effective change requires years. In fact, significant changes and equally significant results can happen in one hundred days. A school science fair provides a great way to celebrate the conclusion of every 100-day cycle and identify what worked and what did not work. Although leaders should certainly consider including national and international research, the use of local results from real students, real teachers, and real schools has the greatest possibility of transforming skeptics into supporters of the professional practices that will work best for their schools.

We now turn our attention to how 100-day leaders can specify the results that will define their success and build momentum for continuous improvement.

Step 6: Specify Results

When educational leaders specify results, they are usually talking about student performance on test scores. These results fall into three essential categories.

1. **Achievement against a standard:** For example, "80 percent of students in grades 3 through 8 will perform at or above grade level in reading."

2. **Achievement compared with other students, schools, or districts:** For example, "80 percent of students will achieve

scores in the 60th percentile or higher when compared with a national norming group," "100 percent of schools will perform above the state average in mathematics performance," and "Our district will rank in the top 20 percent of districts in the state."

3. **Growth:** For example, "Average reading scores will be at least 5 percent higher than last year," "The school will rank at least three positions higher in the state than last year," and "The district will rank higher in the state than last year."

Each of these measurements of results has serious problems. The following sections express the challenges with traditional result measurement; offer a better way to measure and report results for students, schools, and districts; and share common objections to interim assessments. Every measurement has potential error, and the most fair and accurate way to present results is with an understanding of what those errors might be. These challenges are not an argument against measuring and reporting results; rather, they are a call to make that reporting accurate and complete.

The Challenges With Traditional Result Measurement

The first measurement, achievement against a standard, is the least problematic. It sets a clear objective, and the benchmark—80 percent of students will meet or exceed the state standard—does not move. The problem in practice, however, is that state standards are not consistent and clear. This variability occurs because state standards have changed and continue to do so. Starting in the 1990s, and continuing in the early 2000s, each state adopted its own standards. Then many states shifted to the Common Core State Standards. Then many states shifted back again. A standard is a moving target. Even more problematic is the fact that states change tests in both content and format. Even when the standards remain consistent, changes in test format occur (from multiple-choice to open-response and from pencil-and-paper to computer-based testing). In addition, some states change from uniform testing (every student takes the same test for the same grade level) to *computer-adaptive* testing (the items students face vary based on whether they answered the previous question correctly or incorrectly, leading some students to take a test with more difficult questions with content beyond their grade level, and other students to take a test with easier questions, as the computer-adaptive algorithm seeks to identify the grade level at which each student can perform proficiently).

The second measurement, achievement relative to other students, schools, or districts, is even more challenging. This norm-referenced measurement evaluates not how proficient a student is, but how the student performed when compared with other students. Thus, a student, school, or district could achieve identical performance in two consecutive years but in the first year rank above average and the second year below average, based not on the performance of that student, school, or district, but rather on how other students, schools, or districts performed. Imagine if drivers' or pilots' evaluations worked this way. A student might rate as a proficient driver one year and get a license but the next year, with the same performance, be denied a license because the performance of other drivers and pilots changed. Even worse is the situation when a student performs much worse the second year—he or she would objectively fail the driver's and pilot's tests—but he or she is nevertheless awarded the licenses to fly and drive simply because other student drivers and student pilots performed even worse. Imagine such students saying, as their cars and planes endanger their communities, "At least we weren't as bad as those other students!"

As absurd as this seems, it is precisely what happens when leaders and policymakers engage in relative performance. No one knows his or her performance until he or she can see the performance of other students and schools. This is amusing in the context of end-of-season baseball rankings. "Chicago may make the playoffs, but only if Boston loses and Kansas City wins." Note well that Chicago's fate has nothing to do with the team's own success on the field; it only depends on the performance of other teams. This is an interesting statistical game when looking at baseball teams in the fall, but it's a lousy way to evaluate students, schools, and districts.

The third method of measuring results with growth has potential and is explicitly encouraged by the Every Student Succeeds Act (ESSA; 2015), but in most cases, it is deeply fraught with error. Schools most commonly measure growth by comparing students in this year's fifth-grade class with students in last year's fifth-grade class. On the surface, we call this *year-to-year comparison growth*, but such a simplistic measurement fails to recognize that in almost every case, this year's fifth-grade students and last year's fifth-grade students are entirely different students. Perhaps in a very large district with very large numbers, one could make the case that each year is representative of the students and that year-to-year variation does not matter. But the smaller the district, school, and classroom, the greater the impact on year-to-year variation in student performance. Not only does this method measure different students but also in many cases—especially in districts with large percentages of students from low-income families—a very high degree of teacher turnover occurs, and teacher turnover has an epically negative effect on student performance. How significant is the impact of turnover? We analyzed data from a large urban district, and two unmistakable conclusions emerged. First, schools with higher poverty rates have higher turnover of teachers. Second, the relationship between high teacher turnover and low student achievement is significantly greater than the impact of socioeconomic status on student achievement. Although several sophisticated and expensive growth models purport to show student growth over time, the plain fact is that the longer the time period under consideration, the greater the impact of other variables on student achievement. Three years in the life of a student brings not only changes in teachers—a critical impact on student achievement—but also changes in family structure, student physical and cognitive development, and many other factors that influence student achievement. These factors are not necessarily related to the teaching and leadership variables that leaders and teachers seek to understand when talking about educational results.

Traditional measurement systems leave teachers and administrators cynical. Case after case, we have seen how teacher, school, and district ratings vary significantly—from an A to a C and vice versa—based on tiny changes in student performance. An entire district's grade could change based on the performance, presence, or absence of fewer than five students. Classroom teachers, with the same teaching practices, curriculum, assessment, and professional activities, can shift from highly effective to ineffective, based on changes in only a few students' scores. And it's essential to remember that student scores reflect several years of teachers, not merely the teacher from the current year. Third-grade reading scores have their genesis not in the fall of third grade, but in the literacy development techniques that began in kindergarten and the presence or absence of books in the home years before that. Results mean nothing if community members, parents, teachers, and leaders do not perceive the measurements purporting to show results as credible. The good news is that accountability systems can be improved.

A Better Way to Measure Results

Almost every district we have studied has a robust interim assessment system—that is, districts administer assessments in the fall, winter, and spring that, for the most part, allow leaders to observe the same student within the same year as the teacher, curriculum, assessments, and residential and family structure also stay the same. These tightly contained measurements, within two 100-day segments, allow leaders to more accurately, but not perfectly, assess real student growth, while most outside factors that bedevil multiyear comparisons remain constant. In this tightly controlled growth model, educators simply take students where they are and observe growth.

When evaluating fifth-grade students, for example, it doesn't matter if they enter in the fall reading at a second-, fifth-, or seventh-grade level; the measurement of results depends on how each student grows. Leaders may want to set individualized targets for these students—for example, they may set a significantly greater growth target for the students who enter fifth grade at a second-grade level than for the students in the same class who enter reading at a seventh-grade level. The essential leadership decision, however, is that every student must grow, and must do so within a tight time frame that holds the teachers and leaders responsible for those students reasonably accountable.

Objections to Interim Assessments

Teachers and administrators make two common objections to the use of interim assessments to show academic growth. The first and most persistent is that students are already over-tested, and interim assessments simply add to that burden. This is a fair statement in many schools, and we offer a constructive response. Students are over-tested but under-assessed. The distinction is a critical one. Most tests, particularly the most common high-stakes tests administered in the spring, have no educational value for students or instructional value for teachers; results come long after students have finished their school year. Therefore, students cannot use those results to understand how to set individual objectives for improving their learning, and teachers cannot apply the results to their teaching. Leaders can celebrate or bemoan the results, but they have little in the way of constructive action that they can take, other than request that they receive information from the tests in a timelier manner.

Assessments, by contrast, are designed to provide not only a measurement of student achievement but also an immediate and specific guide for improving achievement for each student, classroom, and school. The results of assessments administered early in the school year can provide information that leads to immediate intervention and enrichment and suggest specific enhancements to the curriculum. Educators can assess the effects of those responses to the early-year assessments less than one hundred days later using midyear assessments. That same process of measurement, analysis, and response by students, teachers, and leaders occurs in the winter, and educators can assess the results of those midcourse corrections in the spring, again in fewer than one hundred days. By the end of the year, leaders know real growth for every student, and they feel highly confident in the relevance of these measurements because they reflected growth by the same students with the same teacher within the same year. If leaders are willing to establish this regimen of fall, winter, and spring interim assessments, we advocate that they seek waivers from traditional state and provincial testing in order to report student achievement more accurately. But even without such waivers, these interim assessments provide much more valuable feedback so that leaders can improve teaching, learning, and leadership every one hundred days.

The second objection to interim assessments is that they lack the psychometric properties tests created by states and provinces, and often contracted to national testing corporations, possess. More specifically, commercially created tests often claim to have higher reliability coefficients than locally created interim assessments. It is worth taking a moment to dissect this claim and how much leaders should weigh the claim in their decision making about student testing.

Reliability reflects consistency, and it's a very important property for any scale. After all, if you step on a scale and one day it says 150 pounds, the next day 120 pounds, and the next day 180 pounds, you won't have much luck monitoring your weight because the scale is inconsistent—it's not reliable. In the context of student tests, educators expect consistency among items; if a student gets most items right in geometry, then educators expect that he or she would also get other similar items right, and if a student gets most items wrong in reading comprehension, then educators expect that he or she would also get other similar items incorrect. While this is certainly true in theory, three factors also influence the reliability of a test: (1) the number of items, (2) the sample size of the students taking the test, and (3) the dispersion of results among students. In general, a test with fifty items will have a higher reliability coefficient than a test with twenty-five items, even if the quality of the items is the same. For this reason, many high-stakes tests are unnecessarily long. In pursuit of higher reliability coefficients, test designers subject students—including very young ones—to test fatigue. When a nine-year-old sits in front of a computer or holds a pencil for two hours (and we have witnessed much longer exams), this pursuit of psychometric perfection is misguided. When students lose focus, concentration, and patience, tests measure not real learning but endurance and compliance.

More than 70 percent of school districts in the United States have fewer than 2,500 students (Pelletier, n.d.). Even if the items are of identical quality, most local interim assessments will have lower reliability coefficients than tests provided by testing corporations that have larger sample sizes. This reflects not the test's quality but the number of students taking the test.

The third challenge with reliability, however, is the greatest. Not only do reliability coefficients depend on higher numbers of test items and higher numbers of students, but this calculation also depends on a dispersion of results—the classic bell curve, with a few students on the left, many in the middle, and a few on the right. But if educators' objective is student growth, then one would expect that distribution to change from fall to winter and spring. If teachers and students work very diligently and results improve throughout the year, the spring will have less dispersion of results than the fall. Most leaders and teachers would agree that's a good thing, but they must also prepare themselves for a critic to claim that the spring test has a lower reliability measurement than a test created by a national testing company. That is true, but we believe that is a very sensible trade-off for leaders to make so they have tests that they can use to make better teaching and leadership decisions. To this criticism, 100-day leaders will say, "We don't need a reliability coefficient of 0.9 if it gives us a set of unusable and irrelevant results. While we want the very best assessments we can have, our priority is usable information and a focus on student improvement. Therefore, we will accept a lower reliability coefficient in order to have fewer test items; less test fatigue; fewer students, reflecting the reality of our schools and district; and less dispersion of results. This will more accurately reflect the growth that our students make during the year."

When 100-day leaders consider results, they reflect on not just test performance but also attendance, behavior, teaching practices, and leadership practices. Real results are not merely a set of scores but also a holistic set of measurements that allow leaders to understand where they are and where they are going, and to make decisions throughout the year to improve opportunities for students.

Step 6 asks you to consider the various ways in which educational leaders evaluate student results. We discussed the limitations that standards-based tests, norm-based tests, and growth models have in showing results. We offered a constructive alternative—interim assessments that show growth within the same year—and we anticipated the objections to interim assessments that leaders might hear from their critics.

Summary

In this chapter, we introduced the six steps of 100-day leadership: (1) identify your values, (2) take an initiative inventory, (3) make a not-to-do list, (4) identify 100-day challenges, (5) monitor high-leverage practices, and (6) specify results. It is essential to note that these six steps are not an event, but a continuous process that will help leaders and the schools they serve gain focus, reduce distractions, and most importantly, improve teaching and learning throughout the system.

In the next chapter, we illustrate these six steps with a picture of a 100-day leader in action.

CHAPTER 3

THE 100-DAY LEADER IN ACTION

MARISSA JOHNSON IS a fourth-generation educational leader with
deep roots in her community. Her great-grandmother was a teacher
and her grandfather, a superintendent of the segregated school system
she attended as a child. She grew up hearing tales of how schools
remained segregated long after the U.S. Supreme Court decision
Brown v. Board of Education of Topeka in 1954. Although the unan-
imous decision required desegregation to occur with "all deliberate
speed," many schools in the community remained deeply segregated
well into the 1960s.

And when at last the schools were integrated, the school boards
consolidated the white and black systems and required students from
African American neighborhoods to attend expanded schools that
previously served white students. In a move replicated not only in
the Southern states but also throughout the United States, the consolidated board then closed most of the historically African American
schools, eliminating the jobs of many African American teachers and
administrators. Dr. Johnson's grandfather was offered the opportunity
to retire, but it was an early and forced retirement, and Dr. Johnson
can recall the deep sense of humiliation and betrayal her grandfather
suffered. "This is victory?" he asked in his melancholic recollections
with his family. Dr. Johnson's mother survived the purge of African
American teachers solely because she had a rare skill—teaching mathematics to middle school students.

The entire family knew that dedication and self-sacrifice were noble but insufficient, and they all grew weary of the public admiration of teachers while the daily disrespect from many quarters—from legislators, school board members, parents, and their own students—intensified. Nevertheless, Dr. Johnson eagerly followed in her grandfather's and mother's footsteps and began her teaching career at the same middle school where her mother had taught. From her start as a rank beginner to her positions as department chair and administrator, her career grew, until it stalled. After a frustrating few years of growing demands and little recognition, Dr. Johnson left the district to pursue more money and, importantly, more respect.

After serving as a senior administrator in a neighboring district for five years, she was recruited to become the superintendent of the same school district where three previous generations of Johnsons had served as educators and leaders. The demographics of the district had changed, and a majority of the students—and a majority of the board—were African American. Although the community retained a strong commitment to honest work and entrepreneurial spirit, the statistics told the story of declining wealth and economic opportunity. More than half the students qualified for free or reduced-price lunch, and the unemployment rate among parents was twice the state average.

Although the schools were fully integrated, Dr. Johnson quickly noticed in her building and classroom visits that segregation was as persistent as it had been in the days before the *Brown* decision. The advanced placement and International Baccalaureate classes were overwhelmingly white. Special education classes were overwhelmingly African American, as were dropouts and truant and suspended students. No category of student results mirrored the community population. Dr. Johnson concluded that equal opportunity and integration are illusions if the minute students cross the threshold of the schoolhouse doors, they step back in time fifty years into a segregated world.

Identifying Your Values

Dr. Johnson had participated in strategic planning processes in which large groups of people spent a year or more working on mission, vision, and values. She had a sense of urgency and knew that neither she nor the students of her district could wait a year to get started. Besides, the district already had a set of values that seemed quite reasonable. The problem was that the district had values in name only and did not use these values to guide daily work. The district claimed to believe in these values that her predecessor, the leadership team, the board, and the community had roundly supported. So rather than restart the process, Dr. Johnson decided to make the following existing values come alive.

- "Equality of opportunity for all students"
- "Respect for people, property, and law"
- "Excellence in all that we do"
- "Safety for children and staff"

Dr. Johnson would surely have expressed the values in a different way, as she favored clarity and precision, but she knew that a new leader would get much further by building on the district's strengths rather than by attempting to throw out values in which the community had already invested. Her job was not to ask, "What are our values?" but rather to ask students, staff, and board and community members, "How close are we to living our values?"

Surprised at the prevailing belief among stakeholders that the school system conformed to its values, Dr. Johnson sought voices that had not been heard from when the values were established. Rather than summoning student leaders to her office, she sought out groups of students, going to local gyms, skateboard parks, and other places where students routinely gathered. Rather than listening only to long-established community leaders, she sought out parents in church basements, at community centers, and at neighborhood gatherings. "I'm here not to give a speech," she reassured the students and parents, "but to listen. I just want to know if we are living our values of equality, respect, excellence, and safety."

The responses were tentative at first, but soon swelled to a wave of stories, evidence, and uncontroversial data. Along with a small team, including another senior administrator, two building principals, two teachers, and two parent leaders, Dr. Johnson invested several days in intensive listening. From students, she heard:

- "My brother Freddie is fourteen years old and doesn't know how to read, and he's on the honor roll. They just push him along because nobody wants to deal with it."

- "I got an invitation from a college to apply for admission, and when I asked the counselor for help, he said I was wasting my time."

- "I'm really trying to do the right thing and work with my black friends," said a white sophomore, "but nobody sits together at lunch, nobody studies together, and we're not in any of the same classes. The skate park is the only place we can hang out. And safety? You've got to be kidding. There are hallways in that school where there are never any adults, and we just don't go there."

- "Some of the teachers really go the extra mile to help us, but for others, it's just sink or swim—if we don't get it, then it's always our fault."

From parents, Dr. Johnson heard deeply troubling comments, including:

- "My daughter is named Marissa, too, and she was so proud when you became superintendent. She was an A and B student, always on the honor roll. And she got a scholarship to college. So, everybody was happy for her.

We borrowed more than 20,000 dollars to get her to college and thought she had it made. But she didn't last more than three months. Being on the honor roll in this district doesn't mean anything, at least for our children. She couldn't do college work, didn't know how to ask for help, and was just overwhelmed. She'll be waiting tables for twenty years to pay off that debt."

- "When our two boys were sent to the principal's office for fighting, the school said that they had a behavior disorder, an emotional disorder, and I don't know what else. So now they are in special education classes, where they just try to keep the lid on. I'm not making excuses for fighting—they were wrong, and I let them have it at home. But they're boys who had been sitting all day long and had just had enough. Now school for them is just a prison."

- "I know the teachers mean well. Some have even come to visit our home, and I really appreciated that. But that was just two teachers out of the many my children have had from kindergarten through high school."

Dr. Johnson listened to scores of such comments, including some very positive ones about the commitment of the staff, the courtesy of the secretaries, and the kindness of administrators. However, the overall picture did not illustrate the values the district claimed as its anchor.

Taking an Initiative Inventory

Based on these conversations, Dr. Johnson suspected that the district's schools did not have many programs to help underperforming students. But she found quite the opposite to be true. They had dozens of intervention programs—before school, after school, and on Saturday. They had safety programs, antibullying programs, and behavioral support programs. They spent hundreds of thousands of dollars on antiracism programs and other workshops designed to improve equity in the schools. Special education consultants had come and gone. And the walls of the schools were covered with posters—often defaced—about themes of respect, excellence, teamwork, and so on. Astonishingly, principals had gone their own way on all these interventions, spending the budgets that had been allocated for their schools.

There were no inquiries as to these programs' effectiveness, but based on her preliminary observations, Dr. Johnson determined that the programs were little used and, not surprisingly, had little impact. The students most likely to go to the after-school programs, for example, were not the students who were failing and could not read their assignments or understand the course requirements, but the B students attempting to improve their grade to an A. Some programs had publications that occupied shelves but remained shrink-wrapped, the resources never used. Among the seven schools in the district, Dr. Johnson identified no fewer than eighty-two separate initiatives at the school level, and another thirteen at the district level. Although the schools purchased them all based on the claim that they were "research based" and had "proven results," they appeared to have little to no evidence of impact in the Oak Grove School District.

Making a Not-to-Do List

Dr. Johnson returned to her office to find an avalanche of messages, emails, and texts. Courteous and attentive to others, Dr. Johnson never took out her smartphone during meetings, a practice that allowed messages to pile up with the apparent expectation that she would devote hours to responding to each one. Two board members had left messages with the subject line reading, "Second Request," when they had made their first request just an hour earlier. This district had a culture in which some thought the superintendent's primary job was not to engage with students and parents, as Dr. Johnson had been doing, but to instantly respond to board demands.

Working with her assistant, Dr. Johnson started a list on the whiteboard in her office of every task that was traditionally assigned to the superintendent. They quickly ran out of whiteboard space and continued writing on poster-sized paper that eventually covered her office. She soon realized how her predecessor had, in his words, felt so "overworked and underloved." He regularly worked sixteen-hour days, yet the staff and board members complained that he was unresponsive and a poor communicator. No matter how hard he worked trying to meet people's expectations, the demands always exceeded the time he had available.

Dr. Johnson had heard of successful superintendents who simply stopped answering emails, delegated all responses to other central office leaders, and invested their time in personal meetings and calls. But those superintendents had far more central office administrators than she did. It also surprised her to learn the number of standing committees and task forces of which the superintendent was a member. Her predecessor had devoted as much as thirty hours a week to meetings, certain that he had to attend every meeting, or else people would feel that he was not sufficiently interested in vital matters. He was always the first one in the building and the last one out, and routinely met with parents who were unhappy with a report card and teachers who were unhappy with a principal or department head.

Dr. Johnson decided to start a very important part of focusing her efforts: the not-to-do list. After about forty-five minutes of reviewing the tasks and emails, she came up with the following list.

- "I will not respond to emails or texts during meetings and conferences. I will allocate thirty minutes at the beginning, middle, and end of the day for this purpose—no more."
- "I will not respond at all to emails that cc or bcc the superintendent. My assistant will set up a rule for incoming email that diverts all cc'd mail to a separate

folder. Unless it is addressed to me personally, I will not respond. Moreover, my assistant will review my email inbox and delete emails and unsubscribe to the dozens of email lists that are solicitations or otherwise not directly related to my role as superintendent."

- "When I notice a theme that is consistent among many emails, I will create a single response to that issue, create a hashtag for it, and tweet my response one time. This ensures that everyone—board members, parents, students, and community members—gets a consistent response to the issues important to them, and that I write one message, not twenty-five, to address a single issue."

- "I will not attend any meeting that is designed for information sharing. Unless the meeting includes deliberation and decision making, the superintendent does not need to attend. For meetings I must attend, such as cabinet meetings and board meetings, I will establish a discipline of *deliberation only*—no presentations or PowerPoints. Members will be expected to read materials before the meeting and focus valuable meeting time on inquiry, deliberation, debate, and decision making."

- "I will eliminate the traditional *superintendent's day* events at schools—orchestrated visits that simply take time from teachers and principals and never give the superintendent an authentic view of the school. I will commit to unannounced visits to schools, including classroom visits, at least once per week."

- "I will not meet with parents unless they have first taken their issue to the people responsible—the teacher and principal in the school. If the parents are still not satisfied, I will always make time to meet with parents and students, but only if they have first attempted to resolve the issue with the appropriate people. Similarly, I will not meet with staff members until they have first attempted to resolve their issue with their principal."

- "I will not do tasks that can be handled by my very capable assistant."

In just the first review of the comprehensive task list, Dr. Johnson removed 25 tasks, which had exceeded 150. She knew that she had more to do, but this was at least a good start.

Identifying 100-Day Challenges

Dr. Johnson identified just three 100-day challenges: (1) attendance, (2) D and F rates (she deliberately did not focus on *passing* because she knew that too often a D grade is technically passing, but students who receive Ds are nowhere close to proficiency), and (3) literacy performance.

1. **Attendance:** "First," Dr. Johnson thought, "the students need to show up. We have students and parents who believe that attendance is not important, and part of that is our fault. When students are tardy and truant, nobody cares. Our extracurricular activities are great, but if we have students only coming to school to play football in the afternoon and not coming to class, that is unacceptable."

   Dr. Johnson instigated what she called *sixty-second meetings* for every school. One minute after the tardy bell rang, she required a stand-up meeting in the principals' offices in which every absent student would receive a personal call from a school administrator, a counselor, an administrative person, or anyone else who was not responsible for in-person instruction. This replaced the robocalls that were typically done in the afternoon and ignored, and the calls that the administrative assistant responsible for attendance did. These well-meaning efforts had been designed to reach out to parents, but the attendance data made clear that these efforts had no substantive impact on truancy and tardiness.

Dr. Johnson participated in some sixty-second meetings herself. Imagine parents' surprise when they received a call from Dr. Johnson's cell phone—so the caller ID did not reflect the high school or district—and heard this greeting: "Hello, Ms. Jenkins. This is Dr. Johnson from Oak Grove School District, and we really missed your daughter this morning. Is there anything I could do to help her get to school on time?"

Some parents were confused. "I know that she left here— are you telling me that she didn't go to school?" Some parents were appreciative. "Thank you so much, Dr. Johnson. He'll listen to you, because he won't listen to me." And some were angry. "You have no right to tell me how to raise my kids. We're doing the best that we can, so butt out." But Dr. Johnson persisted, making call after call. Within twenty minutes, every tardy or truant student realized that someone at the school knew his or her name and noticed he or she was absent.

This is not a happily-ever-after story. This emphasis on attendance will continue for years, but in one hundred days, schools reduced chronic absenteeism and tardiness by more than 80 percent. Students just needed to know that somebody cared. While the district had much work to do in curriculum, assessment, feedback, and parental engagement, at least Dr. Johnson got students in their seats, and within one hundred days, she showed that remarkable accomplishments could occur.

2. **Grades D and F rates:** Dr. Johnson also identified a few other 100-day challenges. For example, she found that ninth-grade science had a student pass rate of only 36 percent. Within one hundred days, she instituted common quarterly assessments and implemented the PLC process. These were decisions based on her observations of other urban schools that had experienced significant improvements in student performance when they used common formative assessments and implemented the PLC process. She also required that the science teachers offer early final exams—a transformative change from grading as punishment ("If you don't pass this final, you will fail!") to grading as incentive ("If you pass the early final exams, you will get ten days of freedom and finish this class early"). With the same final exam, same students, and same faculty, the student pass rate increased from 36 percent to 69 percent in one semester. While 69 percent passing certainly fell far below what Dr. Johnson expected, this represented a dramatic improvement in student performance. And she did this in one semester—ninety days.

3. **Literacy performance:** Dr. Johnson knew from the evidence that, of all the professional practices teachers might consider, nonfiction writing offered exceptional returns on the investment of time. So, she asked entire schools to ask students—just once per month, so hardly an imposition on academic freedom—to engage in nonfiction writing.

She stopped the English department from suggesting a full-page, complex, six-trait writing rubric. "Just make it simple," Dr. Johnson insisted. The faculty coalesced around a simplified writing that included claims, evidence, and assessment of the evidence's credibility. This worked for science, social studies, mathematics, and literacy.

While the new writing rubric was far from perfect, Dr. Johnson established, in a single semester, the expectation that every student, in every grade, would do nonfiction writing and receive feedback on his or her nonfiction writing. Although she could think of many other high-leverage strategies she had learned in professional development conferences, it seemed that this one simple and easy-to-understand strategy would have the greatest impact.

Monitoring High-Leverage Practices

Dr. Johnson had seen new leaders attempt to implement too many changes too quickly, followed by cynicism and opposition by teachers who felt overwhelmed. Therefore, she focused on only three professional practices that she expected administrators to monitor.

First, she required common formative assessments, at least once per quarter. This meant that if there were five eighth-grade mathematics classes all with different teachers, at least four times per year, all of those students had the same assessment that the teachers collaboratively scored. She did this because it was imperative that the same level of rigor and high expectations occurred in every class and did not vary wildly from one classroom to the next. Second, she required monthly nonfiction writing assessments in every class. Teachers used the simplified rubric and were free to choose any writing prompt that they wanted in order to integrate the writing assignment with their curriculum. Third, Dr. Johnson asked for a four-line email at the end of every collaborative team meeting, with each line corresponding to one of four critical questions (DuFour et al., 2016) that PLCs must address.

1. **Learning**—What do we want students to learn?
2. **Assessment**—How will we know if they learned it?
3. **Intervention**—What will we do if they have not learned it?
4. **Extension**—What will we do if they already have learned it?

She was not asking for detailed minutes of every meeting— just four quick sentences to explain how the collaborative teams addressed these questions.

Specifying Results

Finally, Dr. Johnson's 100-day leadership plan included identifying results. She very bluntly told her board and stakeholders, "Stalin had five-year plans, and that didn't work out very well. And too many school systems promise five- or seven-year results. I'm not going to do that." And she shared that they would do the following within the next one hundred days.

- "We will improve average daily attendance from 83 percent to 90 percent. That's not good enough for me, but it's a start."
- "We will improve ninth-grade mathematics achievement by 50 percent. That's not good enough for me, but it's a start."
- "We will improve parent participation in our teacher meetings from 20 percent to 50 percent. That's not good enough for me, but it's a start."

And so, Dr. Johnson continued. She simultaneously encouraged and challenged her colleagues and her community. She agreed to monitor these results, and she pledged that, within one hundred days, she would hold herself publicly accountable for progress.

The final chapter of Dr. Johnson's story has yet to be written. She will have triumphs and failures. Some of the students in her district will achieve conventional success and become lawyers, doctors, or professors. And with her exceptional commitment and leadership by example, one of her children or grandchildren will join the next generation of Johnsons who help the school district achieve the promise of excellence and equity that Dr. Johnson's grandfather fought so hard, and sacrificed so much, to achieve.

We now turn our attention to part 2, "Creating the Environment for Success." We begin with a discussion of what we regard as the best hope for creating such an environment: PLCs. While we recognize that education has no silver bullets or magic pills, the PLC process certainly includes some practices that consistently have a positive impact on student results and professional interactions among teachers and administrators. The evidence is clear that collaborative teacher teams working within a PLC represents the single best and most effective way for schools to address the challenges they face.

Summary

In this chapter we illustrated a case of a 100-day leader in action. For leaders new to their position, like Dr. Johnson, there is often a very brief honeymoon period, and then stakeholders expect to see results. Dr. Johnson focused on a few key strategies to improve professional practices and show gains in student results. She was disciplined not only about her own focus but also about helping school administrators and teachers identify the key leverage points that would help them improve student performance. And true to the hallmark of a 100-day leader, Dr. Johnson was able to report to her community how professional practices and student results had improved within one hundred days of when she began her leadership journey. We now turn our attention to how leaders can create the environment for success in every school.

CREATING
THE ENVIRONMENT
FOR SUCCESS

CHAPTER 4
A STRONG FOUNDATION

IMAGINE FOR A moment that you are seeking help from a professional person, perhaps a doctor, lawyer, or contractor. You would expect the professional to use the best practices available; a doctor would use the most effective medicines and instruments, a lawyer would prepare and file all the correct paperwork for your case, and a contractor would use safe, quality materials according to the latest recommendations. Professionals have an ethical obligation to continually seek out and use new and better practices when they have proven more effective than previous ones. Professionals also demonstrate a sharp focus on the purpose—the *why*—of the work, and they do so with passion. These traits are the hallmark of PLCs, and why school leaders must begin embedding the concepts and practices of a PLC during the first one hundred days if the school or district is not already on the PLC journey.

The research is clear: the practices inherent in the PLC process offer educators the best hope for ensuring higher levels of learning for all students. But ever-changing fads in education and leadership turnover make it extremely unlikely that schools continue any single initiative for years. Indeed, in the early stages of even the most promising initiative, frustration often sets in: "We tried that, and it didn't work, so let's abandon it and try the next new thing." The error in this reasoning is that these leaders and schools never really fully implement anything; they only reach the early stages of implementation, and without the depth and duration required for successful implementation of any kind, they see little impact.

Effective professional practices—like any skill—take time to develop. That is why it is essential for leaders to persist in the challenging work of things like collaborative scoring, data analysis, and cross-disciplinary writing, to name just a few examples. These practices require focused and concentrated effort, feedback, and repetition. It is not unusual, for example, that the first attempt at collaborative scoring is a failure, with five teachers on a collaborative team having five different ideas about what student work should be called proficient. The answer, we argue, is not to abandon practices because they are difficult, but to embrace them, persist, and with time and effort, become better at these practices.

The research-based practices embedded in schools and districts that function as PLCs are powerful. In fact, they are so powerful that leaders would be committing educational malpractice if they failed to use them. Just as the best seeds will wither when planted in sand or toxic soil, even the best educational initiatives are doomed without an environment that will nurture and encourage healthy growth and change. The 100-day leader faces the challenge of developing a school culture that allows educators and students to flourish.

The Four Pillars of a PLC

The foundation of a PLC rests on four pillars: (1) mission, (2) vision, (3) values (collective commitments), and (4) goals (DuFour et al., 2016). Each pillar asks a different question of educators.

1. **Mission ("Why do we exist?"):** This question helps staff reach agreement regarding the fundamental purpose of the school. This clarity of purpose helps establish priorities and guides decision making. Ensuring that all students learn must be at the heart of a school's mission.

2. **Vision ("What must we become in order to accomplish our fundamental purpose?"):** In pursuing this question, staff attempt to create a compelling, attractive, realistic future that describes what they hope their school will become. Vision provides a sense of direction and a basis for assessing both the current reality of the school and potential strategies, programs, and procedures to improve on that reality.

3. **Values ("How must we behave to create the school that will achieve our purpose?"):** In pursuing this third question, staff seek to clarify the collective commitments they will make to achieve their vision by acting in certain ways. These commitments guide individual and collaborative work.

4. **Goals ("How will we know if all of this is making a difference?"):** This question helps staff identify the targets and timelines and determine their short-term priorities and the steps to achieve benchmarks.

When teachers and administrators have considered these four questions together and reached their collective position on each one, they have built a solid foundation for a PLC.

Mission

The PLC process provides the structures for 100-day leaders to reach short-term goals. But methods are meaningless without the *why*—the purpose and passion essential for effective educational change. Many think that when initiating any significant change effort, leaders should focus on two questions: (1) "What are we going to do?" and (2) "How are we going to do it?" This is not so. Researchers, writers, and organizational theorists contend that the most important and most effective place to start is with the why—by articulating a clear and compelling organizational purpose.

During the first one hundred days, leaders must align the school or district's core purpose—high levels of learning for all students—with expectations and behaviors. Articulating a clear and compelling purpose provides the foundation of why—why we do what we do—and a compelling why focuses on students and their learning (DuFour et al., 2016; Sinek, 2009).

For school leaders, fragmentation can be the mortal enemy of purpose. Consider the mixed messages leaders receive every day: "You must have every student reading at grade level, because if students cannot read, they will have multiple failures in every other subject. Move heaven and earth to get them to read and write at grade level. Spend whatever time it takes, move the schedule around, provide intervention—whatever you need to do—but get those students reading at grade level. It's the most important thing! . . .

"And make sure that you cover every single standard in science, social studies, and mathematics. If you need to cut back on reading time to do that, then do it, because you'll also be held responsible for covering every element of the curriculum and standards. And did we mention that the school board has adopted a mandatory free-enterprise curriculum that we are adding to the school day? And don't forget about the mandatory character education and social and emotional learning curriculum. And there is a mandatory assembly for all students to hear an inspirational outside speaker. Don't forget DARE (Drug Abuse Resistance Education)—because despite the evidence that it has no influence on student drug use, we're required to pull students out of literacy instruction to get DARE training. You won't have any more time in the school day. Just figure it out."

Any teacher or school administrator would confirm that this is not an exaggeration. The mission question gives leaders a tool to avoid fragmentation and keep the purpose clear.

Keep in mind, however, that communicating a school or district's core purpose is not the same as actually taking action. The key for leaders, especially during the first one hundred days, is to consistently connect the *what* with the *why*: "Here's what we are doing, and here's why it's important."

Vision

Although embedding and communicating a mission of high levels of learning for all students in school or district culture is critical, communicating a compelling purpose, even if done with passion, will only have an impact when leaders quickly implement a collaborative process for developing a compelling vision of the future. Leaders must, during the first one hundred days, create an exciting, energizing vision of the future that is clearly better than the current reality. Simply communicating a clear and compelling purpose won't in and of itself sufficiently drive change. The leader must involve others in creating a "recognizable target that beckons, with both meaning and clear implications for behavior" (Eaker & Sells, 2016, p. 58).

A shared vision of the future is not enough. During the first one hundred days, leaders must also build a strong foundation of shared values and collective commitments—at every level within the school or district.

Values

Deep, rich cultural change is driven by the development and use of shared values and collective commitments. Through shared values, an organization finds its meaning, and through shared commitments, people articulate what they are prepared to do in order for the vision and values to become a reality.

Essentially, collective commitments are a pledge that members of an organization make to each other. Importantly, collective commitments are directly linked to a school or district's mission and vision, essentially addressing the question, "If this is our core purpose (mission), and this is the kind of organization we have said we would like to be (vision), then what commitments are we willing to make in order to fulfill our mission and become the school or district we said we seek to become?" In short, members pledge to act in certain ways (DuFour et. al., 2016).

Importantly, leaders also benefit from collaboratively developed, shared commitments. They are able to move from an almost total reliance on their position of power to a position of moral authority. When a leader must confront problematic behavior, he or she is able to say, "I need you to do this, not simply because I'm the boss, but because everyone pledged to commit to these behaviors." Collective commitments enhance internal accountability (DuFour et al., 2016).

Goals

Collaboratively establishing realistic and meaningful goals guides progress. Goals are simply destinations along the larger journey. They address the questions, "What steps are we going to take and when will we take them?"

Collaborative goal setting is essential for 100-day leadership. It is through the goal-setting process that the team, school, or district is able to set meaningful and realistic short-term priorities, and connect these short-term goal cycles to a larger, more long-term vision of the future. Meaningful, data-based goal setting is a powerful tool for closing the gap between where we are and where we've said we want to be. Absent effective goal setting, faculty and staff are left to multiple disconnected activities that are not connected to a coherent whole.

Leading Cultural Change

Leading cultural change is difficult—much more so than making structural changes such as changing school schedules or staff job descriptions. It is especially difficult if leaders don't focus on the right work in the right way. In short, the first one hundred days are critical for beginning the journey to long-term, systemic change.

Daniel Coyle (2018) defines *culture* as a set of living relationships working toward a shared goal. Culture is not something you are,

Coyle argues, but something you do. He documents the impact of positive culture on organizations. A Harvard study of more than two hundred businesses reveals that a positive culture is related to a net income increase of 756 percent over eleven years (as cited in Coyle, 2018). The impact of positive culture, Coyle (2018) finds, is not limited to businesses. Whether the group is a military unit, movie studio, or inner-city school, the power of culture remains consistent.

Focusing On the Right Things

Virtually everyone has a focus; the question for leaders is, "Are we focused on the right things?" The first one hundred days require leaders to focus on those specific things that will have the greatest long-term impact on achieving the organizational mission and vision and that the school or district will need in order to become more effective over the long term—*the right things*.

During the first one hundred days of implementing any initiative or change, leaders must focus their attention with specificity—drilling deep into the right work the right way. Because the central purpose of any school or district is to ensure high levels of learning for all students, leaders must focus all teamwork through the lens of the impact on student learning, as well as adult learning. Teams do this by focusing on critical learning questions for each student, for each skill, and for the adults who teach them. Teams must be crystal clear about what is essential for every student to learn in each course, subject, unit, and lesson, and collaboratively plan for monitoring student learning on a frequent and timely basis. Additionally, teams must address the question of how to respond when students struggle with their learning, as well as how to extend the learning of students who demonstrate proficiency.

The primary structural and cultural change leaders will make during the first one hundred days is they will develop a culture that captures the power of collaborative teams. It becomes essential then for leaders to focus on the work of each team. Because adults, like kids, learn at different rates and in different ways, leaders cannot realistically think that every team will progress evenly. Specificity and fidelity on the part of the leader will enhance specificity and fidelity in teams. We cannot overstate the importance of focusing on the work of each team and stretching each team's aspirations and performance level—task by task. For student learning, *specificity* requires knowing what the standard would look like in student work, if students are successful. The same idea applies to adults; that is, What would the completed task look like if it was completed at a high level of quality? And, importantly, *fidelity* means doing the right work for the right reasons. In the case of schools, ultimately, it means being faithful to the mission of high levels of learning for all students.

Collaborating Where It Counts

Leading the reculturing of organizations and creating a culture of continuous improvement is, in many ways, a performing art, requiring ingenuity. The idea of the solitary leader overcoming overwhelming odds through sheer will and determination is a myth. Although this view of leadership makes for great reading or movies, in most cases, organizational success results from meaningful, focused, collaborative efforts. This is not to discount the contributions of individuals. The key word, however, is *contributions*. Innovation usually results from multiple individual contributions connected by a collaborative process. One-hundred-day leaders recognize this and act on it. They understand that the depth and quality of collaboration will determine the degree of success the school experiences in each 100-day cycle of continuous improvement.

But what does it mean to successfully collaborate? Successful collaboration involves more than mere dialogue or pleasant interpersonal relationships. It is more than frequent communication, newsletters, and emails. It is more than cooperation. DuFour, DuFour, and Eaker (2008) define *successful collaboration* as "a systematic process in which people work together, interdependently, to analyze and impact professional practice in order to improve individual and collective results" (p. 464). This definition contains key words: *systematic, interdependently,* and importantly, *impact* and *results.* It would be difficult to be an effective team absent one of these characteristics. One-hundred-day leaders set out to create meaningful collaborative cultures not because they view collaboration as an inherently good thing; they embed collaboration to impact results.

Making the Case for Collaboration

Few factors will affect the likelihood of success within each 100-day cycle—and beyond—as deeply as the quality of collaboration that occurs throughout the school or district, day in and day out. Virtually no research evidence supports the notion that having administrators, teachers, and support staff work in isolation will most effectively impact student learning levels across all subgroups. On the other hand, since the 1950s, researchers, writers, and practitioners have pointed to the positive impact of collaborative cultures—when collaboration is done well.

We also know that engaging in work they find meaningful motivates people. And it enhances motivation and the likelihood of success when they do meaningful work in collaboration with others. Besides the fact that developing collaborative cultures to make work more meaningful and success more likely is a worthwhile endeavor, in the 21st century world, collaborative endeavors are a necessity. Warren Bennis and Patricia Ward Biederman (1997) point out:

> In a society as complex and technologically sophisticated as ours, the most urgent projects require the coordinated contributions of many talented people. Whether the task is building a global business or discovering the mysteries of the human brain, one person can't hope to accomplish it, however gifted or energetic he or she may be. There are simply too many problems to be identified and solved, too many connections to be made. (p. 2)

The necessity for meaningful, effective collaborative cultures is no less apparent for educational organizations. Collaboration, organized and propelled by effective leadership, is a prerequisite for success in schools. Creating a culture of continuous improvement requires leaders to pay attention to both the degree of collaborative learning and the quality of capacity building—enhancing the knowledge and skills of both students and adults (Fullan & Quinn, 2016).

Michael Fullan and Joanne Quinn (2016) aren't alone in their observation. Consider what other researchers have to say about the value of collaboration (DuFour et al., 2016):

- "When groups, rather than individuals, are seen as the main units for implementing curriculum, instruction, and assessment, they facilitate development of shared purpose for student learning and collective responsibility to achieve it" (Newmann & Wehlage, 1995, p. 38).

- "[High-achieving schools] build a highly collaborative school environment where working together to solve problems and to learn from each other become cultural norms" (WestEd, 2000, p. 12).

- "Collaboration and the ability to engage in collaborative action are becoming increasingly important to the survival of public schools. Indeed, without the ability to collaborate with others, the prospect of truly repositioning schools . . . is not likely" (Schlechty, 2009, p. 237).

- "Quality teaching is not an individual accomplishment. It is the result of a collaborative culture that empowers teachers to team up to improve student learning beyond what any one of them can achieve alone" (Carroll, 2009, p. 13).

- "We must stop allowing teachers to work alone, behind closed doors and in isolation in the staffrooms and instead shift to a professional ethic that emphasizes collaboration.

We need communities within and across schools that work collaboratively to diagnose what teachers need to do, plan programs and teaching interventions and evaluate the success of the interventions" (Hattie, 2015, p. 23).

As this evidence shows, many people believe that collaboration is a good thing and that most organizations should embrace it as part of their overarching culture. Yet there remains a huge gap between acceptance of collaboration in principle and everyday practice in organizational life. Peter M. Magolda (2005) points out, "The extreme ideal of egalitarian exchange, while an espoused model for collaboration, is unlikely to represent an enacted model for collaboration" (p. 19). Bennis and Biederman (1997) concur, noting, "Despite the rhetoric of collaboration . . . we continue to live in a by-line culture where recognition and status are according to individuals, not groups" (pp. 1–2).

Despite decades of research and real-life success stories, the culture of most schools and districts is still characterized by isolation—teachers working by themselves in solitary classrooms, while being asked to do an increasingly difficult job in a society with higher-than-ever expectations. Simply put, such structures and cultures of isolation are a recipe for failure.

One-hundred-day leaders have the critical responsibility to create, develop, and embed meaningful, high-quality collaboration throughout each 100-day cycle and beyond, to the point where collaboration simply becomes the cultural norm—the way we do things around here. As Douglas Reeves and Brooks Reeves (2017) point out, "When multiple minds come together to form a solution, the process may get messy, but the results speak for themselves" (p. 68).

In part, educators are unwilling to embrace the best practice of collaboration because leaders have failed to provide a structural framework within which collaboration can occur. To make collaboration a way of life, schools and districts must embrace the power of collaborative teams as the basic organizing principle and cultural norm.

Ensuring, Rather Than Encouraging, Collaboration

Successfully developing a collaborative culture requires 100-day leaders to act—to move from encouraging meaningful collaboration to embedding systematic structures and daily procedures that ensure deep, rich collaboration focused on improving student learning. The single most essential prerequisite for creating a meaningful collaborative culture is high-quality leadership reflected in specific actions that ensure collaboration. Consider the following example.

Rick DuFour felt excited when he accepted the principal position at Adlai E. Stevenson High School. Stevenson, a large suburban Chicago high school, had a traditional culture—all teachers worked in isolation. Rick was determined to change the culture to one of meaningful collaboration.

Rick often recalled his first faculty meeting at Stevenson in which he shared with the faculty his determination to create a collaborative culture at the school. He made a commitment to the faculty that if any teachers wanted to collaborate with each other and needed time, support, or resources, he would make it happen. All they had to do was ask. If teachers wanted to collaboratively engage in action research, he would support them. Or, if a teacher team wanted to attend a workshop or present at a professional meeting, he would support that type of collaboration too. In short, Rick declared that the days of teacher isolation were over at Stevenson. Rick's vision and promise to support a collaborative culture met with great enthusiasm and applause.

Rick asked his secretary to create a file of staff requests for collaborative initiatives. At the end of the school year, he wanted to provide evidence to the school board of how the culture at Stevenson had changed. But, as Rick often recalled, the file was empty at the end of that first year. Teachers and administrators had not made a single request for support for a collaborative initiative.

At the beginning of his second year as principal at Stevenson, Rick took an entirely different approach. He took time to explain the benefits of a collaborative culture, citing research and cases from other top-rated high schools as examples of best professional practice. Over the summer, he had organized a small guiding coalition of key staff members to assist him in organizing the school into collaborative teams—teams of professionals who taught the same or similar content or shared similar work.

After seeking input and advice, he selected team leaders, and committed resources to provide them and each collaborative team with training. And, most importantly, he shared examples of the work in which he expected teams to engage. He promised to work with all teams to help them get better. His underlying message was, "Let's get started, and then we'll get better."

The experience at Stevenson taught Rick that collaboration by invitation will not work. To develop a collaborative culture, the leader must deliberately and systematically organize and embed collaborative expectations in the daily life of the school or district.

Creating a Shared Understanding of Teamwork

In the past half century, effective organizations of all types have captured the power of collaborative teamwork as the basic structural and cultural building block for success. Peter M. Senge, Art Kleiner, Charlotte Roberts, Richard B. Ross, and Bryan J. Smith (1994) observe, "We are at a point in time where teams are recognized as a critical component of every enterprise—the predominant unit for decision making and getting things done. . . . Working in teams is the norm in a learning organization" (pp. 354–355). One-hundred-day leaders view collaborative teaming as the fundamental organizing structure for how they undertake the work associated with each

100-day cycle, and they do this with a deep, rich knowledge of how effective teams work. They embed collaborative teams in the structure and culture with passion, specificity, and fidelity.

The impact of collaborative teaming will depend on leaders' ensuring that staff use a common vocabulary. For example, staff must understand what *collaborative teaming* is, and importantly, what it is not. Collaborative teaming is much more than simply working together in groups. By organizing staff into collaborative teams, leaders ask members to work interdependently to achieve a common goal for which they hold each other mutually accountable (DuFour et al., 2016).

The words *interdependently, common,* and *mutually accountable* have particular significance. A group doesn't necessarily work interdependently—for example, a group of runners run a marathon, but they do not work interdependently. While each runner has individual goals, the runners have no common goals. Individual runners also don't hold each other mutually accountable; they only have accountability for their own behavior and performance.

When teams engage in each 100-day cycle to improve student learning, they need to have an understanding of specific terms such as *guaranteed and viable curriculum, common formative assessments, summative assessments,* and *collaborative analysis* of student work and learning. One-hundred-day leaders take steps to make sure that everyone shares a deep, rich understanding of frequently used terms. Developing a shared understanding involves utilizing common definitions and *doing* the right work. People gain a deeper understanding through *learning by doing.*

Aligning the Work of Teams Districtwide

Of course, simply organizing into collaborative teams will do little if anything to ensure a positive impact on student learning. In fact, lacking direction and support, teaming can negatively impact student learning levels. Fullan (2001) cautions, "Collaborative cultures, which by definition have close relationships, are indeed powerful, but unless they are focusing on the right things they may end up being powerfully wrong" (p. 67). Teams require a total commitment from leaders to direct, support, and monitor the work and effectiveness of each team—team by team, task by task.

Just as individuals should not be allowed to work in isolation, neither should teams. One-hundred-day leaders embed collaborative teams districtwide, and they understand and communicate how the work of teams at every level interconnects and how teams impact one another. This requires a conceptual understanding, a gestalt of the greater whole. These leaders use every opportunity to communicate this larger picture. They connect the dots so that every team sees how its work contributes to a larger shared goal. Following are the critical teams each district should have.

The School Board and Superintendent Team

Aligning the work of teams begins with the collaborative work of the school board and superintendent team. The success of your 100-day cycles of continuous improvement will greatly depend on the quality of this team's collaborative teaming. This team must set the direction for the district by articulating a few high-impact *SMART* goals (goals that are strategic, measurable, attainable, results oriented, and time bound; Conzemius & O'Neill, 2014). Further, this team must demonstrate the highest standard of teamwork, providing a model for the entire district to emulate.

The school board and superintendent team sets an example by doing the following.

- Collaboratively developing norms or shared commitments the team members will make to each other, the district, and the larger community
- Engaging in data-based decision making and SMART goal setting for each 100-day cycle and beyond

- Gaining shared knowledge through collective inquiry into best practices
- Providing resources and training
- Monitoring the progress of goal attainment on an ongoing basis
- Enhancing the effectiveness of teams within the district, particularly the principal team
- Recognizing and celebrating successes along the way
- Developing plans to continue the team members' own learning and effectiveness

The Central Office Team

Each school district has its own unique history and context. Regardless of the district's size, if a leader expects educators to form teams at the school level, the central office must also form teams. Avoid the appearance of hypocrisy at all costs. If the district office is exempt from teaming, resisters will stir the pot by saying, "Well, if working in teams is so great, why doesn't the district office work in teams?"

The work of central office teams mirrors the work of other teams within the district. To the degree possible, the team should be composed of personnel who have the same or similar responsibilities. The 100-day leader will guide the team in writing and frequently referring to team norms, using the power of data-based decision making, and setting a few high-impact goals for each 100-day cycle, along with engaging in collective inquiry into best practices.

Central office teams often anticipate issues and questions that will likely arise during each cycle. Effective central office teams also recognize their responsibility to enhance the effectiveness of the principal, teacher, and support staff teams as they work to create 100-day winning streaks. In many ways, the success of other teams within the district is linked to the quality of teaming within the central office.

The Principal Team

Successful 100-day leaders recognize the critical importance of the building principal. And they realize that it enhances each building principal's effectiveness when all district principals organize into a collaborative team. In turn, the quality of the principal team directly impacts the quality of teacher teams' work.

Developing a high-performing principal team requires reimagining the work that occurs in traditional principal meetings—the nuts-and-bolts operational meetings that rarely focus on student learning. Successful 100-day leaders communicate such information in other ways, such as by using email or designated informational meetings whenever possible, reserving principal team time for a deep and meaningful focus on student and adult learning.

For example, the principal team focuses on the following.

- Developing team norms
- Collaboratively analyzing and sharing learning data—districtwide, school by school, team by team, and by grade level or subject and course level
- Setting a few goals for each 100-day improvement cycle, along with more long-term stretch goals
- Seeking best practices, both internally within the district and externally from multiple sources, and using these findings to engage in action research and planning for 100-day cycles of continuous improvement

One-hundred-day leaders rely on the principal team to anticipate issues and questions that will likely arise during each work cycle. And, importantly, the team will collaboratively develop plans for proactively addressing concerns and issues. When appropriate, the principal team will also practice and rehearse the tasks that teacher teams will undertake during their collaborative work.

For example, if teacher teams will collaboratively analyze data to focus on the learning of each student, skill by skill, principals should practice doing this prior to engaging teachers in the work. In many schools, teacher teams are typically asked to successfully complete tasks that principals have never experienced themselves. In schools striving for 100-day winning streaks, however, principals first ensure that they understand and can do the work themselves before tasking teacher teams. This increases the principal's credibility with staff, of course, but more importantly, it improves the principal's ability to assist struggling teams.

One-hundred-day leaders take specific steps, such as amending principal contracts, to ensure that each principal clearly understands it is his or her responsibility to enhance the success of each team within his or her building. They realize that the success of each 100-day cycle, like long-term continuous improvement efforts, depends on the work of teacher teams—and the quality of teacher teaming is inextricably linked to the quality of principal teaming. Those who seek to improve the work of teacher teams start by focusing on and improving the work of the principal team.

The School Leadership Team

Just as the principal team forms the primary link between the central office and all the district's schools, the school leadership team forms the primary link between the principal and all the school's faculty and staff. One-hundred-day leaders ensure that each principal organizes, utilizes, and supports a school leadership team that meets on a regular basis—at least twice a month. While the team's core group consists of the principal and the collaborative teacher team leaders, the team might include others, such as the assistant principal.

The work of the school leadership team mirrors the work of the principal team. In other words, the work starts with the school board and superintendent team, is reflected in the central office team, is duplicated and sharpened in the principal team, and becomes embedded in each school through the school leadership team. The principal chairs this team and is responsible for enhancing its effectiveness by engaging the team on a journey of continuous improvement.

Teacher Teams

Collaborative teaming will only make a positive impact on student learning when teams, especially teacher teams, focus on the right things. Organizing schools into collaborative teams is a means to an end, and the end is to help more students learn at higher levels. Teams can accomplish this only when they focus on the right work. Teams should not try to focus on everything, but rather on the highest-priority things that are most likely to impact student learning (DuFour et al., 2016). For 100-day leaders, the secret to success is focus.

Although teacher teams have no hard-and-fast rules or limitations, four conditions together impact their effectiveness. Teams must have the following.

1. An effective team leader
2. Time to collaborate
3. Collaboratively developed norms to govern their work as a team
4. A principal who is committed to stretching the aspirations and performance of each team within the school

School leaders must recognize their responsibility to ensure that every teacher team has an effective leader. It is simply unreasonable to expect a team to be more effective than its leader.

Team leaders need explicit direction. Leaders can provide this with a clear position description that outlines the overall expectations and daily work. Teacher team leaders should also receive direction at the weekly or biweekly school leadership team meetings.

Teacher team leaders also need training. Like students, adults learn at different rates and in different ways. Some team leaders will need more assistance than others, and the same training may not fit the needs of every team leader. Some team leaders can benefit from being paired with another team leader for coaching and feedback. Others may need to attend a workshop to strengthen a specific leadership skill. Ongoing training is essential, and leaders must tailor it to each team leader's individual needs.

Teacher teams will need time within the school day to collaborate. Solutions range from using common preparation time to adjusting the start time or end time of one school day a week. Some schools use banked time, while others rely on group activities or shared classes to allow teams to find collaboration time. Many school leaders find they must first take very small steps to create some temporary time to collaborate; after teams realize that collaboration is positively affecting student learning, the school leaders can then turn to more creative and aggressive means of finding time, such as changing the school schedule.

Teacher teams, like all teams, should collaboratively develop team norms—commitments that team members are willing to make to each other. Team norms reflect the way in which team members will approach their work and the parameters within which work will occur. As DuFour et al. (2016) remind teams:

> When individuals work through a process to create explicitly stated norms, and then commit to honor those norms, they increase the likelihood they will begin to function as a collaborative team rather than as a loose collection of people working together. (p. 72)

Support Staff Teams

Capturing the power of collaborative teaming should not be limited to those who have direct responsibility for teaching and learning within the district. Others, such as the transportation, food service, and maintenance departments' staffs, can benefit from working in high-performing collaborative teams with those in similar roles. Although these teams might adapt their work to realistically focus on the unique aspects of each team's core purpose, the work of these teams will mirror the work of others. They will collaboratively develop and utilize team norms, make data-based decisions, set a few high-impact goals for each 100-day cycle as well as more long-term goals, and continually seek to embed best practices related to their areas of responsibility.

As with other teams, the effectiveness of the support staff teams has a direct link to team leadership, and like teacher teams, support staff teams will need resources, support, and training. Absent effective support staff teams, 100-day leaders will not likely be able to successfully engage in long-term, districtwide continuous improvement.

Focusing Teacher Teams on Learning

Successful leaders limit the work of teacher teams to a few key tasks. They prioritize the teamwork around the four critical questions of a PLC (see page 68; DuFour et al., 2016). If leaders really want all students to learn at high levels, then teams must do the following.

- **Collaboratively clarify the knowledge, skills, and dispositions that every student must acquire as a result of each unit, course, or grade level:** Teacher teams engage in collaborative study to clarify and add meaning to the standards, and to establish high-priority standards. Leaders must expect teams to pace out the instructional calendar, ensuring enough time to teach the high-priority standards, or the more essential parts of standards, first. Teams must drill deeper into each standard by asking, "What would this standard look like in student work, if the standard was met?" and "What would proficiency look like?" They then sharpen the standards by developing learning targets, followed by student *I can* statements—the essential outcomes written in student-friendly language so that students can monitor their own learning.

In short, leaders must ensure that each teacher team engages in collaboration that results in *a guaranteed and viable curriculum* focused on enhancing student learning (Marzano, Warrick, Sims, & Heflebower, 2014). This means the curriculum is focused enough so that all teachers can address it in the time available, and all students can learn the critical content of the curriculum in the time available. Once the team has identified essential content, individual teachers do not have the option to disregard or replace it.

- **Collaboratively determine how the team will know when each student has acquired the essential knowledge and skills:** The most powerful strategy teams can utilize to monitor student learning on a frequent and timely basis is team-developed formative assessments. These team-made assessments—intended to measure only the high-priority learning expectations—are essential to monitor the learning of each student, skill by skill, on a frequent, timely, and ongoing basis.

  Formative assessments differ from summative assessments in that the team uses the information it gleans from a collaborative analysis of formative assessment results to provide students who are struggling with additional time and support, and to ensure that students who demonstrate proficiency are challenged by extending their learning. The team also uses this information to reflect—both individually and as a group—on the effectiveness of current instructional practices.

  Douglas Reeves (2004) refers to common teacher-made formative assessments as the "best practice in assessment"

(p. 71) and the "gold standard in educational accountability" (p. 114). Because common formative assessments are so powerful, 100-day leaders do not leave their use to chance. They provide the expectation, rationale, training, monitoring, and ongoing support to ensure teacher teams harness the power of common formative assessments to improve student learning.

- **Collaboratively develop a plan to respond when students experience difficulty learning:** A key question that drives 100-day leaders is this: "Are students learning, and how do we know?" Students learn in different ways and at different rates. In every unit of instruction, some students will have trouble with some skill or concept. Most schools leave it to individual teachers to help those students, and many teachers work hard to do so. However, an individual teacher can only do so much. Even with the best of intentions, individual teachers quickly reach his or her limit when it comes to providing all students with the necessary additional time and support to succeed.

  Effective principals work with staff to collaboratively develop a schoolwide system of interventions that ensures students can receive additional time and support within the school day, regardless of the teachers to whom they are assigned. DuFour et al. (2016) propose that an effective plan for additional time and support will reflect specific characteristics. Because the plan for additional time and support is schoolwide, it is a systematic process, and it is timely; students don't wait until late in the school year to get help. The plan is directional, rather than invitational; it directs students to get assistance, rather than simply encouraging them to do so. It is flexible; students are not labeled—they move in and out of interventions as needed.

Merely having a plan for a schoolwide system of interventions does not suffice. Leaders must aggressively monitor the plan's effectiveness.

- **Collaboratively develop a plan to extend the learning of students who demonstrate proficiency:** Effective leaders realize their job is not merely to ensure that all students learn at minimally acceptable levels. They strive to create a culture of continuous improvement for all students—and adults. Because of their commitment to higher levels of learning, they engage teachers in developing a systematic plan that will extend the learning of students who demonstrate proficiency.

  This requires a shift from an ability-based culture to an effort-based one. When Rick DuFour was principal at Stevenson High School, one of the United States' most celebrated and recognized high schools, he and his faculty made this commitment to all students: "If you will undertake a more rigorous and challenging curriculum, we will provide you with the additional time and support to help you be successful in the course of study you choose."

Planning Units of Instruction

As teachers engage in the teamwork associated with a collaborative learning culture, it only follows that they should collaboratively plan units of instruction, too. In addition to the benefits gained by consistency, teachers also benefit from learning from each other.

One-hundred-day leaders are not obsessed with unit plan formats. They are obsessed with the quality of the discussions and thought processes that go into developing plans for instruction. They make sure that the conversations focus on the right questions (the critical questions of a PLC) and teachers use data, seek best practices, and always work to answer the question, "How can we best ensure all students learn the right things at a high level?"

The quality of unit planning is directly linked to the quality of dialogue. What should drive discussions when teachers are planning common units of instruction? Many have found figure 4.1, in which Robert Eaker and Janel Keating (2012) graphically adapt the work of Larry Ainsworth and Donald Viegut (2006), helpful.

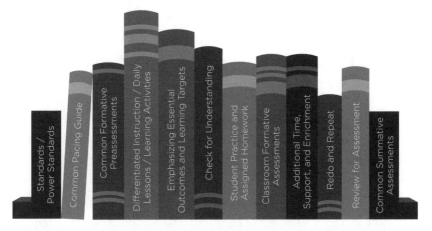

Multiple Checks for Understanding During the Unit

Performance • Product / Rubric Scoring • Pencil-and-Paper Assessments • Observation

Source: Eaker & Keating, 2012. Adapted from Ainsworth & Viegut, 2006.

Figure 4.1: Unit planning—A conceptual framework for teams.

This "bookshelf" is, at its core, a way of thinking. Teacher teams in the White River School District in Buckley, Washington, widely use it. Teachers first discuss each bookend to clarify the standard and the end-of-unit summative assessment. They ensure that what the summative assessment asks students to do to demonstrate proficiency is consistent with expectations associated with the standard.

Teachers then discuss questions such as the following.

- "How much time have we allotted for this unit?"
- "Are the students ready for this content?"
- "How can we best differentiate instruction?"

- "How will we emphasize learning targets and check for understanding?"
- "What will be the most appropriate things to practice, both in class and at home?"
- "When will we give our common formative assessments?"
- "How will students access additional time and support, and what are the conditions for students to rework?"
- "How can we best review with students prior to the summative assessment?"

These are not the only things teacher teams will or should discuss when developing common unit plans, of course; rather, they are simply examples of how to guide the discussion. Effective teams make sure they don't make the plans so tight that teachers can't bring their own individual expertise into their classrooms. Some schools also find it helpful to plan a certain number of weeks around common units of instruction while leaving a couple of weeks open for makeup time, special units, and so on.

Each team should keep a notebook containing its work—for example, the team's norms, curriculum guides, common formative assessments, unit plans, and unit reflections captured after the team delivered the unit. When team members begin planning a unit of instruction, they turn to their notebook and review the previous year's plan and unit reflections. Teams usually find that they have already done most of the work associated with unit planning; they only need to revisit the unit plan and embed the suggested changes the team recorded the previous year.

Importantly, teams should post the products they produce—such as unit plans—online on the school or district's central server. Adults can learn in a very meaningful way by examining each other's work—especially the work of others within the same school or district. In short, 100-day leaders create a culture of transparency in which the primary work of each team is available for others to see.

Analyzing Student Work and Learning

Effective leaders ensure a sharp focus on the learning of each student, skill by skill, by having teacher teams collaboratively analyze data and student work. A collaborative analysis of formative assessment results, if done with specificity and fidelity, provides teams with important, actionable information. First, teams can identify, for each skill, which students demonstrated proficiency and which students require additional time and support. They can then discuss the teaching patterns and materials that led to success and think of ways to build on those instructional techniques, and they can identify interventions for students who need them.

The collaborative analysis of formative assessment results also allows teams to reflect on the effectiveness of their own instructional practices, to learn from each other, and to project how they might teach various skills differently the next time. In short, collaborative analysis of student learning specifically provides learning information about each student, as well as information about group and individual instructional effectiveness.

As teacher teams collaboratively analyze formative assessment results, 100-day leaders ensure teams also analyze the accompanying student work. This is critical. For example, suppose three students miss the same two mathematics problems on a test; by looking at their work, the team might discover that they missed the problems for different reasons and need varying interventions to ensure specific prerequisite skills. The point is this: teams must do collaborative analysis student by student, skill by skill, rather than student by student, problem by problem.

Monitoring and Celebrating the Work of Teams

Leaders must be sure to monitor the work of teams. Most obviously, they can do this by frequently reviewing student learning data.

They can also monitor and support teams' work in a powerful way by examining the various products teams develop, such as curriculum guides, unit plans, and formative assessments. Effective 100-day leaders ensure quality teamwork by first doing the following.

- Ensuring teams understand why each team product is important and where it fits in the larger efforts to improve student learning
- Providing exemplars of what the work should look like
- Engaging teams in the collaborative development of quality standards

This should send a clear message from leaders: "We need you to do this. Here's why. Here's how it fits other efforts. Look at these examples of the quality your work should meet. You'll receive this training and support, and we'll provide additional assistance, as needed, along the way." Spending some time setting up teams for success will make ongoing teamwork faster and better.

Effective leaders also realize the importance of recognizing and appreciating teams' hard work. They build specific plans for publicly recognizing and celebrating the work of teams into each 100-day cycle. Two words are key: (1) *plans* and (2) *publicly*. Recognition as an afterthought will have little to no impact. As Rick DuFour was fond of saying, "Hoping for small wins is not the same as planning for small wins." And, if recognition and celebrations do not occur publicly, they will have little impact on the individual or group being recognized, and no impact on others. The power of frequent, meaningful, public recognition and celebrations lies not simply in the impression they make on the recognized person or group, but in the message they send to others. The message says, "See what these people have accomplished? It can be done, and we very much appreciate it. If they can do it this well, you can do it too!"

Summary

The ability to create 100-day winning streaks has a direct link to the quality of the school or district's foundation. Using the PLC process to embed powerful elements like the collective mission, vision, values, and goals and creating an effective collaborative culture ensure that leaders achieve short-term wins for long-term success. One-hundred-day leaders must possess a deep knowledge of collaborative teaming practices and commit to supporting the work of each team within each 100-day cycle. This requires both specificity and fidelity. Although building the foundation and embedding collaborative teaming throughout a school or district can be difficult and time consuming, they are not only inherently worthwhile but also essential to success in student learning.

E. D. Hirsch Jr. (2016–2017), writing in *American Educator*, declares:

> If I were a principal in a primary school, I'd spend my money on teachers, on their ongoing development, and on creating conditions in which the work of teachers in one grade supports the work of teachers in the next, and in which teachers would have time to consult and collaboratively plan. . . . Good teaching can often depend more reliably on the coherence of the wider system, and the cooperation it brings, than on virtuoso performances. (p. 33)

The necessity of a collaborative culture and, more specifically, collaborative teaming is not a new story. The question facing the 100-day leader is not, "Should our school organize into collaborative teams in order to succeed in each 100-day cycle?" but rather, "How will I effectively lead collaborative teams, day in and day out, as we strive to fulfill our core purpose of ensuring high levels of learning for all students?"

CHAPTER 5

HOW TO BEGIN FROM WITHIN

MAKING A SIGNIFICANT impact during the first one hundred days requires a leader to first look inside, examining his or her own beliefs, assumptions, and behaviors before looking to others and articulating what they need to do. Effective leaders begin from within. Tasha Eurich (2018) provides powerful evidence that effective leaders must reflect and have self-knowledge. Her seven-day insight challenge allows leaders to understand their motivations, strengths, and challenges before they attempt to mediate others (Eurich, 2018).

In this chapter, we consider both personal beliefs and the specific actions leaders take that reflect those beliefs. Leaders must link who they are to what they do. Leaders have an obligation to create a sense of home—for both students and adults—which leads to self-efficacy and optimism, compared with pessimism and despair.

Hendrie Weisinger and J. P. Pawliw-Fry (2015) find that adults and children who have more hope have higher levels of satisfaction, self-esteem, optimism, meaning in life, and happiness. They cope better with injuries, diseases, and pain. Hope is a better predictor of future personal and professional success than either intelligence or natural ability.

Auditing Your Assumptions

Leadership effectiveness, especially during the critical first one hundred days, greatly depends on leaders' beliefs and assumptions, which drive the way leaders think and, more importantly, how they act. Examine your beliefs and assumptions using the following questions.

- "What things will I be tight about—what are my non-negotiables?"
- "What assumptions do I have about leading others and human motivation and how I can lead most effectively?"
- "What assumptions do I have about those with whom I will be working? What assumptions do I have about human interactions?"
- "What assumptions do I have about the organization's core purpose and what it should become?"
- "What assumptions do I have about students, their parents, and the larger community?"
- "What assumptions do I have about monitoring, publicly recognizing, and celebrating the success of others?"

Possessing an Optimistic Mindset

A leader's impact during the first one hundred days will depend not only on the leader's assumptions but also on the leader's sense of optimism and the belief that he or she can, in fact, succeed. Much has been written about the importance of leaders having high expectations of those around them. But before leaders can impact those around them with high expectations, they must have high expectations of themselves. Self-efficacy is contagious, and furthermore, a collaborative culture enhances it. Collaborative teams enhance the likelihood of success, and cycles of success enhance each team member's sense of self-efficacy; team members believe, "We can do this!"

Modeling What You Expect of Others

At its core, *leadership* means modeling the behavior that the leader expects of others. Leaders who first look inside must ask the all-important question, "Am I prepared to demonstrate the same attitude and behaviors that I will expect others to show?" In this section, we provide rubrics leaders can use to assess six dimensions of leadership: (1) resilience, (2) personal behavior, (3) student achievement, (4) decision making, (5) communication, and (6) learning.

Resilience

Figure 5.1 presents a rubric for use in assessing a leader's resilience.

1—Not Meeting Standards, 2—Progressing (Leadership Potential), 3—Proficient (Local Impact), 4—Exemplary (Systemwide Impact)	
1. Constructive reaction to disappointment and failure	
4	• The leader's public reports, including accountability documents, plans, and oral presentations, include frank acknowledgment of prior personal and organizational failures and clear suggestions for systemwide learning resulting from those lessons.
3	• The leader readily acknowledges personal and organizational failures.
2	• The leader acknowledges personal and organizational failures when confronted with evidence.
1	• The leader is defensive and resistant to acknowledge error.
2. Willingness to admit errors and learn from them	
4	• The leader shares case studies of personal and organizational errors to guide, inspire, and teach colleagues throughout the organization. • The leader builds resilience in colleagues and throughout the organization by habitually highlighting and praising "good mistakes," where people took risks, made mistakes, and learned lessons, and both the individual and the organization learned for the future.
3	• The leader admits errors quickly, honestly, and openly with his or her direct supervisor and immediate colleagues. • The leader shows evidence of learning from past errors and willingly accepts feedback and discusses errors.
2	• The leader is able to accept evidence of errors when others offer it. • Some evidence shows that the leader learns from mistakes.
1	• The leader is unwilling to acknowledge errors. • When confronted with evidence of mistakes, the leader is defensive and resistant to learn from mistakes.

Figure 5.1: Resilience leadership rubric. continued →

3.	Constructive handling of disagreement with leadership and policy decisions
4	• When disagreements with leadership and policy decisions occur, the leader can articulate the disagreement and advocate for the organization's best interest, and willingly and appropriately challenges executive authority and policy leaders with evidence and constructive criticism. But once organizational leadership and policy decisions are made, the leader fully supports and enthusiastically implements the decisions.
3	• The leader accepts and implements leadership and policy decisions.
2	• The leader sometimes challenges leadership and policy decisions without bringing those concerns to appropriate executive and policy authorities. • The leader sometimes implements unpopular policies unenthusiastically and says, "I'm just following orders, but I don't like it."
1	• The leader ignores or subverts leadership and policy decisions that are unpopular or distasteful.
4.	**Constructive handling of dissent from subordinates**
4	• The leader creates constructive contention, assigning roles if necessary to deliberately generate multiple perspectives and consider different sides of important issues. • The leader recognizes and rewards thoughtful dissent. The leader uses dissenting voices to learn, grow, and, where appropriate, acknowledge the leader's error. • The leader encourages constructive dissent by hearing and encouraging multiple voices. This results in a better and more broadly supported final decision.
3	• The leader uses dissent to inform final decisions, improve the quality of decision making, and broaden support for final decisions.
2	• The leader tolerates dissent, but very little of it occurs in public because subordinates do not understand the leader's philosophy about the usefulness of dissent.
1	• Dissent is absent due to a climate of fear and intimidation.
5.	**Explicit improvement of specific performance areas based on previous leadership evaluations**
4	• The leader combines previous leadership evaluations with personal reflection and 360-degree feedback to formulate an action plan that is reflected in the leader's daily priorities and in the organization's priorities. • Previous evaluations influence not only the leader but also the entire organization.

3	• The leader explicitly reflects previous leadership evaluations in projects, tasks, and priorities. • Performance on each evaluation reflects specific and measurable improvements along the performance continuum, from ineffective to progressing, to proficient, to exemplary.
2	• The leader is aware of previous leadership evaluations, but has not translated them into an action plan.
1	• The leader's chosen tasks and priorities have no evidence of or reference to previous leadership evaluations.

Visit **go.SolutionTree.com/leadership** for a free reproducible version of this figure.

Personal Behavior

Figure 5.2 presents a rubric for use in assessing a leader's personal behavior.

1—Not Meeting Standards, 2—Progressing (Leadership Potential), 3—Proficient (Local Impact), 4—Exemplary (Systemwide Impact)	
1. Integrity	
4	• The leader meets commitments—verbal, written, and implied—without exception. • Commitments to colleagues, students, community members, and subordinates have the same weight as commitments to superiors, board members, and other people with visibility and authority. • The leader's commitment to integrity is clear throughout the organization, as any commitment from anyone who reports to this leader is as good as a commitment from the leader.
3	• The leader meets commitments or negotiates exceptions where someone cannot meet a commitment. • Verbal commitments have the same weight as written commitments.
2	• The leader meets explicit written commitments. • The need to "get it in writing" does not allow subordinates or superiors to assume that verbal statements have the weight of a written commitment.
1	• The leader regards the words "I'm working on it" or "I'm doing the best I can" as acceptable substitutes for commitments. • The leader cannot be trusted to follow through with tasks, budgets, priorities, or performance.

Figure 5.2: Personal behavior leadership rubric.   continued →

2.	Self-control
4	• The leader possesses complete self-control, even in the most difficult and confrontational situations, and also assists colleagues on techniques of emotional intelligence. • Not only does the leader exemplify emotional intelligence but also the entire organization reflects this commitment to self-control, empathy, and respect.
3	• The leader can deal with sensitive subjects and personal attacks with dignity and self-control. • The leader never meets anger with anger, but defuses confrontational situations with emotional intelligence, empathy, and respect.
2	• The leader occasionally raises his or her voice when angry or threatened. • The leader leads a climate in which people are reluctant to raise sensitive issues.
1	• The leader loses his or her temper and is emotionally unstable. • Conversations on any sensitive topic are brief or nonexistent.

3.	Compliance with legal and ethical requirements in relationships with employees
4	• The leader meets the letter and spirit of the law, avoiding both the fact and the appearance of impropriety. • The leader inculcates the foundations of mutual respect for colleagues and respect for the law throughout the organization.
3	• The leader has no instances of illegal or unethical conduct with employees or prospective employees, or other conduct that crosses the line of policy or law.
2	• There is no progressing in this leadership dimension—one strike, and you're out. Failing to have proficiency is the same as being ineffective.
1	• The leader violates—even just one time—the legal and policy requirements for the relationship between leaders and employees.

4.	Compliance with legal and ethical requirements in relationships with students
4	• The leader teaches faculty and students respect for one another, creating a climate for mutual trust and respect. • The leader builds an environment in which all employees and faculty members know student safety is paramount and inappropriate contact with students never occurs.
3	• The leader meets all legal requirements for student contact and takes swift and appropriate actions when inappropriate contact between employees and students has been detected.
2	• There is no progressing in this leadership dimension. A single violation is a career killer.
1	• The leader fails to protect student safety by permitting or engaging in inappropriate contact with students.

5.	Tolerance of different points of view within the boundaries of the organization's values and mission
4	• The leader actively seeks differences in perspective, encouraging different scenarios and curricula in the context of academic standards. • The leader explicitly differentiates constructive divergent thinking that facilitates a transition to convergent thinking to support organizational goals.
3	• The leader focuses evaluation on the achievement of the mission and adherence to values, without penalizing differences in points of view that fall within organizational requirements.
2	• The leader does not punish alternative points of view, but does little or nothing to develop or encourage those views.
1	• The leader suppresses other points of view and discourages disagreement or divergent thinking.
6.	Organization of calendar, desk, office, and building
4	• The leader maintains a daily prioritized task list that he or she can spontaneously produce at any time. • The leader keeps his or her desk clean with the highest-priority work on the desk and other work in pending files. • The leader keeps his or her calendar openly available, free of conflicts, and focused on the leader's and the organization's priorities. • The building is spotless and reflects the leader's commitment to a personal sense of pride. All administrators and teachers keep their desks clean, calendars consistent, and task lists visible and in priority order. • The grounds, building, restrooms, lounges, public areas, and especially classrooms reflect the leader's sense of dignity, order, and decorum.
3	• The leader always has his or her daily prioritized task list and up-to-date calendar available. • The leader keeps his or her work space flawlessly organized.
2	• The leader can make his or her calendar and task list available when given warning. • The leader keeps his or her work space tolerably but imperfectly organized. • The rest of the building does not reflect a commitment to organization and discipline.
1	• The leader has no task list and an outdated calendar. • The leader's desk is messy. • The building, public areas, classrooms, and other physical facilities are a mess.

Visit *go.SolutionTree.com/leadership* for a free reproducible version of this figure.

Student Achievement

Figure 5.3 presents a rubric for use in assessing a leader's proficiency in leading student achievement.

1—Not Meeting Standards, 2—Progressing (Leadership Potential), 3—Proficient (Local Impact), 4—Exemplary (Systemwide Impact)	
1. Planning and goal setting for student achievement	
4	• The leader routinely shares specific leadership, teaching, and curriculum strategies that are associated with improved student achievement. • Other leaders in the system credit the leader with sharing ideas, coaching teachers and leaders, and providing technical assistance to implement successful new initiatives.
3	• The leader's student achievement goals and strategies reflect a clear relationship between teachers' and other leaders' actions and student achievement. • Results show steady improvements based on these leadership initiatives.
2	• The leader has established specific and measurable student achievement goals, but these efforts have yet to result in improved student achievement.
1	• The leader's student achievement goals are neither measurable nor specific. The leader focuses more on student characteristics than on the actions of the teachers and leaders in the system.
2. Student achievement results	
4	• The leader has a consistent record of improved student achievement on multiple indicators of student success. • Student success occurs not only overall but also in each group of historically disadvantaged students. • Data indicate that the leader has improved student performance. • In areas of previous success, the leader aggressively identifies new challenges, moving proficient performance to the exemplary level. • Where new challenges emerge, the leader highlights the need, creates effective intervention, and reports improved results.
3	• The leader hits the numbers, meeting student performance goals. • The student population average improves, as does the achievement of each group of students whose data have previously identified as needing improvement.
2	• The leader has some evidence of improvement, but insufficient evidence of changes in leadership, teaching, and curriculum that will create the improvements necessary to achieve student performance goals.

1	• Indifferent to the data, the leader blames students, families, and external characteristics for student achievement. • The leader does not believe that student achievement can improve. • The leader has not taken decisive action to change schedules, teacher assignments, curriculum, leadership practices, or other variables in order to improve student achievement.
3.	**Student achievement reporting to students, parents, teachers, and other leaders**
4	• Reports at all levels extend far beyond the report card and include standards achievement reports, detailing student performance on the most important standards. These reports include power standards, which teachers identify as most related to student performance at the next instructional level. • Faculty meetings and professional development meetings focus on the locally produced academic reports, and clear evidence shows changes in leadership, teaching, and curriculum in response to these analyses. • Leaders can produce academic achievement reports at any time, and for students who require particular assistance, they increase the frequency of academic achievement reporting.
3	• Student achievement reports include not only traditional report cards and grades but also standards achievement reports, detailing student performance on standards, as part of each reporting period.
2	• The school delivers required report cards in a timely and accurate manner. • Faculty members and administrators can explain the relationship between grades and standards where required.
1	• The school provides standard report cards with letter grades. • Any relationship between grades and standards is a matter of the teacher's individual discretion.
4.	**Use of student achievement data to make instructional leadership decisions**
4	• Clear evidence shows that the leader has used state or provincial, district, building, and classroom data to make specific and observable changes in teaching, curriculum, and leadership. • The leader regularly shares with other leaders and teachers both successes and failures based on local data analysis. • The leader makes a data wall the focal point of both formal and informal leadership and faculty discussions.
3	• Clear evidence shows that the leader has made changes in curriculum, teaching, and leadership based on data. • The leader has a data wall, and both the leader and teachers refer to it in order to inform instructional decisions.

Figure 5.3: Student achievement leadership rubric.

continued →

2	• The leader participates in data-driven decision-making workshops, but limited evidence shows that the leader has made data-based changes.
1	• The leader is indifferent to data and makes no changes in scheduling, instruction, curriculum, or leadership compared with the previous year. • The data scream, "Change!" and the leader's actions say, "Everything is just fine."

5. Understanding of student requirements and academic standards	
4	• Faculty members use the power standards and share them with faculty members in other buildings. • Every faculty meeting and staff development forum focuses on student achievement, including reviews of individual student's work compared with standards.
3	• The leader has analyzed each academic standard and translated it into student-accessible language. • Faculty members widely share power standards and make them visible throughout the building. • The leader makes the link between standards and student performance evident by posting proficient student work throughout the building.
2	• The leader has posted standards. • The leader has conducted the required training.
1	• The leader leaves classroom curriculum as a matter of individual discretion. • The leader hesitates to intrude on or is indifferent to classroom decisions that vary from academic standards' requirements.

6. Understanding of student performance levels based on consistent assessments that reflect local and state or provincial academic standards	
4	• Evidence shows that the leader has made decisive changes in teacher assignments and curriculum based on student performance data. • The leader widely shares case studies of effective and ineffective decisions with other leaders and throughout the district.
3	• Evidence shows that the leader has made specific changes based on student performance data.
2	• The leader is aware of the need to change, but he or she has not yet implemented changes.
1	• The leader is indifferent to the need for change—unable or unwilling to make difficult decisions.

7.	Decisions in teacher assignment, course content, scheduling, and student curriculum based on specific student achievement needs
4	• The leader uses multiple data sources, including state or provincial, district, school, and classroom assessments, and has at least three years of data. • The leader systematically examines data at the subscale level to find strengths and challenges. • The leader empowers teaching and administrative staff to draw inferences from data. • Data insights are regularly the subject of faculty meetings and professional development sessions. • The leader can specifically document examples of data-based decisions in teacher assignment, curriculum, assessment, and intervention. • The leader has coached leaders in other schools to improve their data-analysis skills.
3	• The leader uses multiple data sources, including state or provincial and district assessments, and has at least two years of data. • The leader systematically examines data at the subscale level to find strengths and challenges. • The leader can specifically document examples of data-based decisions in teacher assignment, curriculum, assessment, and intervention.
2	• The leader is aware of state or provincial and district results and has discussed those results with staff, but has not linked specific decisions to the data.
1	• The leader is unaware of or indifferent to the data.

*Visit **go.SolutionTree.com/leadership** for a free reproducible version of this figure.*

Decision Making

Figure 5.4 presents a rubric for use in assessing a leader's proficiency in decision making.

1—Not Meeting Standards, 2—Progressing (Leadership Potential), 3—Proficient (Local Impact), 4—Exemplary (Systemwide Impact)
1. Factual basis for decisions (including specific reference to internal and external data on student achievement and objective data on curriculum, teaching practices, and leadership practices)
4 • The leader makes decisions not by consensus or leadership mandate but based on data. This adherence to the rule of data is reflected in all decisions, ranging from course and classroom assignments to the discontinuation of programs.

Figure 5.4: Decision-making leadership rubric. continued →

	• The leader can cite specific practices that he or she has changed, discontinued, or initiated based on data analysis. • The leader uses a variety of data sources, including qualitative and quantitative data. • Data sources include state or provincial, district, school, and classroom data. • The leader widely shares data inferences and data analysis with others outside the school community so they can replicate the leader's success.
3	• The records of decision making reflect a clear reliance on state or provincial and district student achievement data.
2	• The leader makes some decisions based on data, but he or she makes others as a result of personal preference or tradition.
1	• The leader rarely uses data to make decisions; the predominant decision-making methodology is either a popularity contest or an imperial mandate from the leader.
2. Clear decision-making structure (including which decisions the staff make by consensus or independently, which decisions the leader makes after getting input from the staff, and which decisions the leader makes alone)	
4	• All stakeholders understand the different decision-making levels (where level 1 represents a staff decision by consensus or majority, level 2 represents a decision requiring staff input that will significantly influence leadership decisions, and level 3 represents a unilateral leadership decision). • The leader uses data in such a compelling way that the vast majority of decisions are level 1 decisions. • Staff surveys reflect that staff feel empowered and personally responsible for organizational success.
3	• The leader clarifies the decision-making method for major decisions and shares decisions with the staff, using data to the greatest extent possible to support those decisions.
2	• The leader uses both consensus and unilateral decision making, but he or she does not consistently make the reason for changing decision-making structures clear.
1	• The leader lurches from autocracy to democracy with no clear decision-making method, demoralizing and bewildering the staff.
3. Decisions linked to vision, mission, and strategic priorities	
4	• The leader makes the organization's vision, mission, and strategic priorities visible; ingrains them in the organization's culture; and routinely uses them as a reference point for decisions. • The leader uses strategic decision-making guidelines to make many decisions self-evident and avoids unproductive arguments.

3	• The leader's decisions are consistent with the organization's vision, mission, and strategic priorities.
2	• While the vision, mission, and strategic priorities may be visible, the leader does not consistently link them to his or her decisions.
1	• The leader is unaware of or disconnected from the organization's vision, mission, and strategic priorities. There is little to no evidence of a relationship between leadership decisions and these organizational guideposts.

4. Decisions evaluated for effectiveness and revised where necessary	
4	• The leader can provide clear and consistent evidence of decisions that have changed based on new data. • The leader regularly does decision reviews and *sun setting* in which he or she re-evaluates previous decisions in light of the most current data. • The organization has a culture of *honest bad news* in which the leader and everyone in the organization can discuss what is not working without fear of embarrassment or reprisal.
3	• The leader has a record of evaluating and revising decisions based on new information.
2	• The leader has new information and appears willing to reconsider previous decisions, but does not have a clear record of making changes.
1	• The leader is mired in old decisions, accumulating each one as if decisions were etched in stone. Little to no evidence shows that he or she reflects on and re-evaluates previous decisions.

*Visit **go.SolutionTree.com/leadership** for a free reproducible version of this figure.*

Communication

Figure 5.5 presents a rubric for use in assessing a leader's proficiency in communication.

1—Not Meeting Standards, 2—Progressing (Leadership Potential), 3—Proficient (Local Impact), 4—Exemplary (Systemwide Impact)	
1. Two-way communication with students	
4	• In addition to having all the proficient characteristics, the leader goes to exceptional lengths to listen to students. The listening strategies may include focus groups, surveys, student advisory committees, and numerous one-on-one student conversations. • Discussions with students reveal that they know the leader will listen to them and treat them with respect.

Figure 5.5: Communication leadership rubric. continued →

3	• The leader knows students' names, regularly greets students by name, and proactively talks with and listens to students. • The leader makes him- or herself particularly visible at the beginning and end of the school day and during all other times when students are present.
2	• The leader knows most students' names, often greets students by name, and talks with students frequently. • The leader makes him- or herself visible.
1	• The leader does not know students' names, avoids student contact except where leadership's presence is required, and retreats to the office during most occasions where students are likely to be present. • Many students do not know the leader's name or recognize the leader on sight.

2. Two-way communication with faculty and staff

4	• In addition to having all the proficient behaviors, the leader actively listens to the faculty and staff. • The leader's calendar reflects numerous individual and small-group meetings with staff at every level, not just with the direct reports. Bus drivers, cafeteria workers, and first-year teachers all feel confident that they could get the leader to respectfully hear them out.
3	• Faculty meetings include open two-way discussions. • Faculty members regularly have the opportunity for one-on-one meetings with the leader. • The leader knows all staff members and makes an effort to recognize the personal contribution each one makes.
2	• The leader typically only listens to questions during faculty meetings.
1	• Faculty meetings consist of the reading of announcements and include little to no interaction.

3. Two-way communication with parents and community

4	• There is clear evidence that the leader has engaged in parent- and community-centered communication, including through open forums, focus groups, surveys, personal visits, and extensive technology use. • Decisions in curriculum, leadership, staffing, assessment, and school appearance reflect parent and community involvement. • Survey data suggest that parents and community members feel empowered and supportive of educational objectives.
3	• The leader frequently interacts with parents and community members, including through newsletters, personal briefings, personal visits and calls, and technology use (voice mail, hotlines, email, and websites) where appropriate. • There is clear evidence that the leader has based decisions on input from parents and community members.

2	• The leader gives parents and community members a respectful hearing when they initiate the conversation.
1	• Parents and community members play little to no role in leadership decision making.

*Visit **go.SolutionTree.com/leadership** for a free reproducible version of this figure.*

Learning

Figure 5.6 presents a rubric for use in assessing a leader's proficiency in learning.

1—Not Meeting Standards, 2—Progressing (Leadership Potential), 3—Proficient (Local Impact), 4—Exemplary (Systemwide Impact)	
1. Personal understanding of research trends in education and leadership	
4	• In addition to widely and deeply reading educational research, the leader contributes directly to research, case studies, experimental results, and research questions to serve the interests of other leaders and educational organizations.
3	• The leader engages in personal reading, learning, and teaching of educational research trends.
2	• The leader occasionally reads educational research and has some interest in personal reading and learning.
1	• The leader engages in little to no personal learning and research.
2. Personal professional development plan	
4	• In addition to meeting the requirements for proficient performance, the leader approaches every professional development opportunity with a view toward multidimensional impact. • The leader shares knowledge and skills throughout the organization and with other departments, schools, and districts. • Rather than merely adopting externally generated professional development tools, the leader specifically adapts learning tools so that they are homegrown and become part of the organization's culture.
3	• The leader engages in professional development that is directly linked to organizational needs. • The leader makes building on personal leadership strengths a priority. • The leader personally attends and actively participates in the professional development that is required of other leaders in the organization. • In the case of building principals, the leader personally attends and actively participates in teachers' required professional development.

Figure 5.6: Learning leadership rubric. continued →

2	• The leader actively participates in professional development, but it is reflective of a personal agenda rather than the organization's strategic needs. • The leader attends professional development for colleagues, but does not fully engage in it or set an example of active participation.
1	• The leader might introduce a professional development program but quickly leaves the room, signaling to colleagues that this is not really worth his or her time. • When the leader does engage in personal professional development, he or she will likely go to a national conference selected for its location rather than its content or strategic relationship to organizational needs.

3. Professional development focus	
4	• The leader can identify specific professional development offerings of past years that he or she has systematically reviewed and terminated because they failed to support organizational goals. • The leader has a prior review process for new professional development programs and rigorously applies it to applications for time and funding. • The leader can provide examples of applications for professional development that he or she disapproved because they failed to meet the criteria. • The leader chooses one or two focus areas for professional development; extensive time in faculty meetings, grade-level meetings, department meetings, and staff development meetings focuses on intensively implementing a few learning areas.
3	• The professional development plan has no more than six areas of emphasis, and each area is linked to the organization's strategic objectives.
2	• Professional development opportunities somewhat relate to organizational objectives, but the leader has no way of systematically assessing their impact. • The leader uses participant evaluations as the primary criteria for selection, so programs that are popular but ineffective tend to become the norm.
1	• By personal example, the leader endorses the *butterfly approach* to professional development; once he or she superficially addresses a subject, he or she chases a new fad. • The leader frequently approves faculty requests whether or not they relate to student achievement. • The leader bases his or her personal professional development agenda on whims and preferences, not organizational needs.

4. Application of learning	
4	• In addition to meeting all the criteria for proficient performance, the leader provides evidence of the principle of leverage, applying each learning opportunity throughout the organization. • The leader creates forms, checklists, self-assessments, and other learning tools so that teachers and other leaders apply concepts learned in professional development daily throughout the organization. • The leader regularly shares these application tools with other departments, schools, or districts in order to maximize the impact of the leader's personal learning experience.
3	• There is clear evidence that the leader has actually applied personal learning in the organization. • Where teachers and other leaders have not applied learning within the organization, the leader rigorously analyzes the cause of this and stops investing time and money in professional development programs that lack clear evidence of success in the organization.
2	• The leader has intellectually accepted some important learning experiences but can give only a few specific examples where he or she applied learning to the organization.
1	• Even on those rare occasions when the leader engages in professional development, he or she appears to do it merely to collect information, rather than to reflect on it and apply it to the organization. • Professional development is an expense, not an investment in constructive improvements.

*Visit **go.SolutionTree.com/leadership** for a free reproducible version of this figure.*

Summary

Of course, looking inside at one's beliefs and assumptions, as important as that may be, will have little to no impact on others unless leaders have the passion to act, the courage to keep acting, and the integrity to act for the right reasons, always modeling what they expect from others and keeping an optimistic mindset. During the first one hundred days, leaders must model a sense of passion and excitement. Leadership takes energy. It is virtually impossible for a leader to have success during those critical first one hundred days if he or she assumes the role of the reluctant leader. On the other hand, a leader who is energetic, positive, passionate, and optimistic can positively impact the emotions of others within the district, school, team, or classroom.

EPILOGUE

PUTTING YOUR STARS ON THE TABLE AND MAKING LONG-TERM SUCCESS POSSIBLE

WHEN MILITARY OFFICERS are promoted to general or flag officer, their perspective changes. Rather than commanding a specific group of soldiers, sailors, or airmen—a platoon, company, battery, battalion, or brigade—they now have a broader responsibility to the nation. General officers have an obligation to speak truth to power and not merely to follow orders. As a matter of ethics and long military tradition, they are required to "put their stars on the table" whenever a gap arises between an order and an ethical imperative. School leaders are the general officers of the educational system. When political demands threaten educational imperatives, these educational leaders, like general officers, put their stars on the table, even if it means they might get fired. We have often told superintendents that they cannot choose whether or not to be fired, but they can choose to get fired for the right reasons. There is never any disgrace in losing a job by placing the interests of students first.

School leaders face ethical challenges every day, with the competing demands for achievement, as measured by state or provincial test scores, and care of students. We know of a principal who served a K–8 urban school in which a third of the population was homeless, two students and a parent were killed during a single year, and every day involved the need to feed, clothe, and bathe students. This principal was fired for having low mathematics scores. She could have neglected her students' basic human needs in order to improve test scores. She could have cheated. But she chose principle over job security. She was, in brief, fired for the putting the interests of students first.

Your success as an educational leader is a matter of life and death. According to the Alliance for Excellent Education, students who fail to finish high school have an unemployment rate of over 50 percent, suffer lifelong losses in income, have a higher participation rate in the criminal justice system, and most importantly, have higher illness, injury, and mortality rates than their counterparts who finish high school (as cited in Loschert, 2016).

Kilauea on the island of Hawaii is one of the world's most active volcanos (and may even be at the top of the list); it has erupted several times in the 21st century, spewing molten lava into the Pacific Ocean and decimating entire neighborhoods in the path of the lava flow (USGS, n.d.). Deadly cracks surround the volcano, and each year, tourists die trying to get a better view. Imagine a volcano were on your school grounds and students who "slipped through the cracks" met this horrible fate. That illustrates precisely what happens when students fail. They don't simply slide through the cracks, as if it were a casual accident. They fall, which has life-threatening consequences.

On the one hand, in spite of widespread perception otherwise, U.S. educators are doing better than ever before, with high school graduation rates reaching new highs in 2017 (Balingit, 2017). On the other hand, schools can—and must—do better. In addition to the often-quoted economic, political, and cultural reasons, schools and districts have a moral obligation to do better. During the first one hundred days, leaders must inspire fellow educators and non-educators alike to create districts, schools, classrooms, and even lessons that they consider good enough for their own children. Most everyone knows what a good school, a good teacher, or a good class-room is like. The issue is not a lack of knowledge, but one of will; Do people have the will to create good schools for everyone? This is the leader's job—convincing those around him or her that essential changes in teaching and leadership are possible and that these changes can be undertaken not in years or months, but within days.

The challenges of education in developing countries offer some useful insights for 100-day leaders everywhere. For example, the challenges in the central Africa nation of Zambia can be overwhelming, with more than one hundred students to a class, little or no paper, and schools so crowded that they have three shifts per day of students and teachers. Many of the teachers are teaching in their third or fourth language, as Zambia is a nation with seven official languages. Despite these challenges, there is a genuine zeal for education, even among the poorest rural populations. So after centuries of war, trivial rivalries, and colonialism, what can possibly be done in one hundred days?

Douglas Reeves's brother, Andy, has built schools, clinics, and teacher housing in Zambia. There, he noticed that the buildings alone did not sufficiently attract students—and especially girls—to school. For countless generations, girls had the responsibility to carry water from the stream to their homes, a task that often occupied the entire day. If a daughter's family had to choose between her education and the need for fresh water, education would lose every time. So Andy installed freshwater wells next to the school, allowing the girls to both get an education and provide water for their families. As a result, their school attendance skyrocketed to the point that as many girls enrolled as boys. It may take years to address all of the educational challenges that Zambia faces, but we can dig a well in one hundred days.

What are the "freshwater wells" that your school needs? Food? Technology? A quiet place for students to study and complete homework because they have little to no opportunity to do so at home? Finding your school's "wells" requires you to have a clear vision and focus that you cannot possibly achieve in an environment dominated by initiative fatigue.

Leaders may not be able to solve every problem in the world of education, but they can address the challenges before them in the next one hundred days. A 100-day plan allows for more systemic actions than merely putting out fires and dealing with the crises of the moment. A 100-day plan also prevents leaders from procrastinating through the guise of a plan that focuses only on one-, three-, or five-year goals. One-hundred-day leaders make explicit contributions to results every single day, and the people in the organizations they lead have the satisfaction of knowing that despite occasional disappointments, they are making visible progress every day, with vital goals that help students.

APPENDIX

The 100-Day Plan

You have one hundred days to make a difference. Use the following template to create your 100-day plan.

1. Identify Your Values

Begin with values—your bone-deep beliefs that will prescribe the goals you will, and will not, pursue as a leader.

2. Take an Initiative Inventory

List the leadership and instructional initiatives that your school already has in place. The list is always longer than you think it will be. Take an initiative inventory of everything on your plate. Ask teachers and staff about their perceptions of the initiatives.

3. Make a Not-to-Do List

Before you set your goals for the next one hundred days, identify in specific terms those tasks, projects, priorities, and initiatives that you will not do. Make the list public. Before you ask your staff to implement the 100-day plan, tell them what they can stop doing.

4. Identify 100-Day Challenges

Identify your top-priority challenges for the next one hundred days. Be specific. They might relate to reducing student failure or improving discipline, parental engagement, attendance, or staff morale—you decide. But you must set specific and measurable goals with which you can make an impact in one hundred days.

page 1 of 2

100-Day Leaders © 2019 Solution Tree Press • SolutionTree.com
Visit **go.SolutionTree.com/leadership** to download this free reproducible.

5. Monitor High-Leverage Practices

Identify specific professional practices that you will implement immediately. These need not include major changes, such as adopting a new curriculum or assessment system, but practices that you and the staff can put in place immediately. Examples include the following.

- Effectively monitoring collaborative team meetings within the PLC
- Changing a schedule to allocate more instructional time to areas where data suggest students need more help
- Shifting staff meeting time to allow for collaborative scoring of student work
- Scheduling three common formative assessments in the next one hundred days

In other words, identify short-term, achievable goals whose implementation you can clearly observe.

6. Specify Results

Finally, identify the results that you will measure. Consider how to display these results in an easily understandable visual featuring before-and-after data. Examples of results include the following.

- Reading comprehension
- Writing proficiency
- Mathematics proficiency
- Attendance
- Parental engagement
- Consistency of scoring
- Student engagement

100-Day Leaders © 2019 Solution Tree Press • SolutionTree.com
Visit **go.SolutionTree.com/leadership** to download this free reproducible.

Collaborative Team Rubric

4—Adaptive: Highly Effective Practice, 3—Deliberate: Mostly Effective Practice, 2—Progressing: On the Road to Effective Practice, 1—Emerging: Beginning to Show Signs of Effective Practice

PLC Impact—Norms

4	Each team member has a role (facilitator, recorder, reporter, timekeeper, and so on). Team leaders reference norms at the beginning of each meeting, and the team lives by these norms in every meeting, so much so that the team minimizes time spent on norms.
3	Team members may have roles, but they do not explicitly use them or function within the role descriptions. Team leaders reference norms at the beginning of each meeting, and the team does its best to use these norms in each meeting.
2	Team leaders reference norms at the beginning of each team meeting. Team members may or may not use roles to affect the team's efficiency.
1	The team has some evidence of roles, but it has not yet established norms (agreements on how to resolve conflicts and work as a team) to guide the team. Team members may have serendipitous roles, but the team does not explicitly state or use them for team efficiency.

PLC Impact—Data Use

4	The team uses quantitative and qualitative data based on teachers' and students' most current needs, not adult convenience or administrative directive. Evidence of learning is valid and reliable, and the team has evaluated it for the appropriate level of rigor. Team members perceive data as evidence of learning, rather than mere numbers. The team seamlessly uses relevant data that it can act on in the next few days. The team brings in student work samples that support formative, summative, or performance assessment data. The team prepared data in advance of the meeting to allow more time to discuss instruction. The team splits meeting time between two days. The team disaggregates data by groups for differentiation or response to intervention, which includes relevant student data for targeted instruction.
3	The team uses relevant data that it can act on in the next week. Evidence of learning is valid and reliable, and the team may have evaluated it for the appropriate level of rigor. The team may or may not bring in student work samples that support formative, summative, or performance assessment data. The team may or may not have prepared data in advance of the meeting to allow more time to discuss instruction. The team may split meeting time between two days. The team disaggregates data in some way.
2	The team uses data that it can act on in the next few weeks. The team may be missing student work samples that support inferences made on formative, summative, or performance assessment data. The team may or may not have prepared data in advance of the meeting to allow more time to discuss instruction. The team may split meeting time between two days to allow for data analysis that reveals the strengths and opportunities for growth that inform instruction. The team might disaggregate data, but not in a meaningful or helpful way that supports instruction.

page 1 of 4

| 1 | The team uses data that it can act on, but it does not make the time frame for action clear. The team may be missing student work samples that support inferences made on formative, summative, or performance assessment data. The team may not have prepared data in advance of the meeting to allow more time to discuss instruction. The team does its best in its insufficient time to support data for instruction. The team does not disaggregate data. |

PLC Impact—SMART Goals

4	The team consistently sets focused goals that are strategic, measurable, attainable, results oriented, and time bound. All team members understand how to implement and adjust the goals.
3	The team consistently sets focused goals that match at least four of these elements: strategic, measurable, attainable, results oriented, and time bound. All team members understand how to implement the goals.
2	The team consistently sets focused goals that match two of these elements: strategic, measurable, attainable, results oriented, and time bound. At least three-quarters of team members understand how to implement the goals.
1	The team sets goals that match at least one of these elements: strategic, measurable, attainable, results oriented, and time bound.

PLC Impact—Instructional Strategies

4	The team spends more time (a minimum of two-thirds of team time) focused on instruction—or curriculum standards and resources or assessments that support the instructional process—than on any other part of the PLC process. Any team member who discusses a strategy or intervention clearly conveys the steps necessary to best implement that strategy so that team members can implement it and an observer can potentially observe it as successful. The strategy directly connects to the standards' target level of content and rigor. Strategies are targeted to at least three distinct, differentiated student group needs.
3	The team spends time (a minimum of one-half of team time) focused on instruction, or curriculum standards and resources or assessments that support the instructional process. Any team member who discusses a strategy or intervention conveys most of the steps necessary to best implement that strategy. The strategy connects to the standards' target level of content and rigor. Strategies are targeted to at least two distinct, differentiated student group needs.
2	The team spends time (a minimum of one-third of team time) focused on instruction, or curriculum standards and resources or assessments that support the instructional process. Team members who discuss a strategy or intervention convey some of the steps necessary to best implement that strategy. The strategy may or may not connect to the standards' target level of content and rigor. The strategies may not be targeted to differentiated student group needs.
1	The team sees the need to spend more time focused on instruction, or curriculum standards and resources or assessments that support the instructional process. Team members who discuss a strategy or intervention may or may not convey some of the steps necessary to best implement that strategy. The strategy may or may not connect to the standards' target level of content and rigor. The team only addresses whole-group instruction.

100-Day Leaders © 2019 Solution Tree Press • SolutionTree.com
Visit **go.SolutionTree.com/leadership** to download this free reproducible.

4—Adaptive: Highly Effective Practice, 3—Deliberate: Mostly Effective Practice, 2—Progressing: On the Road to Effective Practice, 1—Emerging: Beginning to Show Signs of Effective Practice

	PLC Impact—Success Criteria
4	The team clearly conceived and communicated the vision for successful use of the strategy so that outside observers would clearly know what to expect (what they'd see and hear from the students and the teacher) and look-fors are easily observed. The success criteria successfully and clearly combine the language of the standards, rigor, and implementation, as well as linear steps for using the strategy.
3	The team clearly conceived and communicated the vision for successful use of the strategy so that outside observers would mostly know what to expect (what they'd likely see and hear from the students and the teacher) and look-fors are tied to the process in some way. The success criteria combine the language of the standards, rigor, and implementation.
2	The team may or may not have clearly conceived and communicated the vision for successful use of the strategy so that outside observers might know what to expect (what they'd likely see and hear from the students and the teacher) and look-fors are tied to the process in some way. The success criteria combine at least two of the following indicators: the language of the standards, rigor, and implementation.
1	Some evidence shows that the team has conceived and communicated a vision for successful use of the strategy so that outside observers might know what to expect (what they'd likely see and hear from the students and the teacher) and look-fors are tied to the process in some way. Emerging evidence shows that the success criteria cite at least one of the following indicators: the language of the standards, rigor, and implementation.

	PLC Impact—Next Steps
4	At the end of its meeting, the team crafts an achievable agenda for the next meeting, indicating actionable future steps for each team member. All members discuss the implementation of agreed-on next strategies or planned practices, and each member discusses the appropriate evidence of student learning he or she intends to bring to the next meeting.
3	As a result of its meeting, the team crafts an agenda for the next meeting, indicating actionable future steps for most team members. Most members discuss the implementation of agreed-on next strategies or planned practices, and most members discuss possible evidence of student learning they intend to bring to the next meeting.
2	The team crafts a possible agenda for the next meeting, which may or may not be an extension of the current meeting, indicating possible next steps for some team members. Some members discuss the implementation of agreed-on next strategies or planned practices, and some members discuss possible evidence of student learning they intend to bring to the next meeting.

100-Day Leaders © 2019 Solution Tree Press • SolutionTree.com
Visit **go.SolutionTree.com/leadership** to download this free reproducible.

1	The team may or may not craft a possible agenda for the next meeting, which may or may not be an extension of the current meeting, indicating next steps for team members. There is some evidence that members have discussed part of the implementation of agreed-on next strategies or planned practices, and perhaps some members discuss possible evidence of student learning they intend to bring to the next meeting.

PLC Impact—Leadership Monitoring

4	A representative team member or team leader meets with the building principal to successfully and articulately convey strategies and success criteria. The meeting is timely, focused, and effective. The principal or administrators follow up with formative walkthroughs to confirm that teachers have implemented the strategy and to observe most of the success criteria (at least three-quarters). The building principal regularly shares the most successful strategies with other faculty in some medium to build capacity, maximizing successful instruction.
3	A representative team member or team leader meets with the building principal to convey strategies and success criteria. The meeting is timely, focused, and effective. The principal or administrators follow up with formative walkthroughs to confirm that teachers have implemented the strategy and to observe most of the success criteria (at least one-half).
2	A representative team member or team leader meets with the building principal to convey strategies and success criteria. The meeting may or may not be timely, focused, and effective. The principal or administrators may follow up with formative walkthroughs to confirm that teachers have implemented the strategy and to observe some of the success criteria (at least one-third).
1	A representative team member or team leader may meet with the building principal at some point after teachers' collaboration time. The meeting may or may not be timely, focused, and effective. The principal or administrators may need to follow up with formative walkthroughs to confirm whether teachers have implemented the strategy and to observe the success criteria.

REFERENCES AND RESOURCES

Advent School. (n.d.). *Learn, act, change: Advent's strategic plan.* Accessed at https://adventschool.org/welcome/strategic-plan on February 4, 2019.

Ainsworth, L., & Viegut, D. (2006). *Common formative assessments: How to connect standards-based instruction and assessment.* Thousand Oaks, CA: Corwin Press.

Alter, J. (2006). *The defining moment: FDR's hundred days and the triumph of hope.* New York: Simon & Schuster.

Archimedes Quotes. (n.d.). *BrainyQuote.* Accessed at https://brainyquote.com /quotes/archimedes_101761 on April 2, 2019.

Balingit, M. (2017). U.S. high school graduation rates rise to new high. *Washington Post.* Accessed at https://washingtonpost.com/news/education /wp/2017/12/04/u-s-high-school-graduation-rates-rise-to-new-high/?utm _term=.b2d8074ac41a on March 26, 2019.

Bennis, W., & Biederman, P. W. (1997). *Organizing genius: The secrets of creative collaboration.* New York: Basic Books.

Berry, L. L., & Seltman, K. D. (2008). *Management lessons from Mayo Clinic: Inside one of the world's most admired service organizations.* New York: McGraw-Hill.

Blanchard, K. (2007). *Leading at a higher level: Blanchard on leadership and creating high-performing organizations.* Upper Saddle River, NJ: Pearson.

Brown, A. (2014). *The myth of the strong leader: Political leadership in the modern age.* New York: Basic Books.

Brown v. Board of Education of Topeka, 347 U.S. 483 (1954).

Carroll, T. (2009). The next generation of learning teams. *Phi Delta Kappan, 91*(2), 8–13.

Champy, J. (1995). *Reengineering management: The mandate for new leadership.* New York: HarperBusiness.

Collins, J. C., & Porras, J. I. (1997). *Built to last: Successful habits of visionary companies*. New York: HarperBusiness.

Conzemius, A. E., & O'Neill, J. (2014). *The handbook for SMART school teams: Revitalizing best practices for collaboration* (2nd ed.). Bloomington, IN: Solution Tree Press.

Coyle, D. (2018). *The culture code: The secrets of highly successful groups*. New York: Bantam Books.

Crenshaw, D. (2008). *The myth of multitasking: How "doing it all" gets nothing done*. San Francisco: Jossey-Bass.

Dalai Lama and Tutu, D. (2016) *The book of joy: Lasting happiness in a changing world*. New York: Avery.

Drucker, P. F. (1992). *Managing for the future: The 1990s and beyond*. New York: Dutton.

DuFour, R., DuFour, R., & Eaker, R. (2008). *Revisiting Professional Learning Communities at Work: New insights for improving schools*. Bloomington, IN: Solution Tree Press.

DuFour, R., DuFour, R., Eaker, R., & Many, T. W. (2010). *Learning by doing: A handbook for Professional Learning Communities at Work* (2nd ed.). Bloomington, IN: Solution Tree Press.

DuFour, R., DuFour, R., Eaker, R., Many, T. W., & Mattos, M. (2016). *Learning by doing: A handbook for Professional Learning Communities at Work* (3rd ed.). Bloomington, IN: Solution Tree Press.

DuFour, R., & Marzano, R. J. (2011). *Leaders of learning: How district, school, and classroom leaders improve student achievement*. Bloomington, IN: Solution Tree Press.

DuFour, R., & Reeves, D. (2016). The futility of PLC lite. *Phi Delta Kappan*, *97*(6), 69–71.

DuFour, R., Reeves, D., & DuFour, R. (2018). *Responding to the Every Student Succeeds Act with the PLC at Work process*. Bloomington, IN: Solution Tree Press.

Eaker, R., & Keating, J. (2012). *Every school, every team, every classroom: District leadership for growing Professional Learning Communities at Work*. Bloomington, IN: Solution Tree Press.

Eaker, R., & Sells, D. (2016). *A new way: Introducing higher education to Professional Learning Communities at Work*. Bloomington, IN: Solution Tree Press.

Education Week. (2018, January 10). *10 big ideas in education.* Accessed at https://edweek.org/ew/toc/2018/01/10/index.html on April 2, 2019.

Elmore, R. F. (2004). *School reform from the inside out: Policy, practice, and performance.* Cambridge, MA: Harvard Education Press.

Ericsson, A., & Pool, R. (2017). *Peak: How all of us can achieve extraordinary things.* New York: Vintage.

Eurich, T. (2018). *Insight: The surprising truth about how others see us, how we see ourselves, and why the answers matter more than we think.* New York: Currency.

Every Student Succeeds Act of 2015, Pub. L. No. 114-95, 20 U.S.C. § 1177 (2015).

Frankl, V. E. (1959). *Man's search for meaning.* Boston: Beacon Press.

Fullan, M. (2001). *Leading in a culture of change.* San Francisco: Jossey-Bass.

Fullan, M. (2008). *The six secrets of change: What the best leaders do to help their organizations survive and thrive.* San Francisco: Jossey-Bass.

Fullan, M. (2018). *Nuance: Why some leaders succeed and others fail.* Thousand Oaks, CA: Corwin.

Fullan, M., & Pinchot, M. (2018). The fast track to sustainable turnaround. *Educational Leadership, 75*(6), 48–54.

Fullan, M., & Quinn, J. (2016). *Coherence: The right drivers in action for schools, districts, and systems.* Thousand Oaks, CA: Corwin Press.

Goleman, D., Boyatzis, R., & McKee, A. (2002). *Primal leadership: Realizing the power of emotional intelligence.* Boston: Harvard Business School Press.

Goodwin, D. K. (2018). *Leadership: In turbulent times.* New York: Simon & Schuster.

Grenny, J., Patterson, K., Maxfield, D., McMillan, R., & Switzler, A. (2013). *Influencer: The new science of leading change* (2nd ed.). New York: McGraw-Hill Education.

Hattie, J. (2009). *Visible learning: A synthesis of over 800 meta-analyses relating to achievement.* New York: Routledge.

Hattie, J. (2015, June). *What works best in education: The politics of collaborative expertise.* London: Pearson. Accessed at www.pearson.com/content/dam/corporate/global/pearson-dot-com/files/hattie/150526_ExpertiseWEB_V1.pdf on February 1, 2019.

Hersey, P., Blanchard, K. H., & Johnson, D. E. (2001). *Management of organizational behavior: Leading human resources* (8th ed.). Upper Saddle River, NJ: Prentice Hall.

Hirsch, E. D., Jr. (2016–2017). In defense of educators: The problem of idea quality, not "teacher quality." *American Educator, 40*(4), 30–33.

Hoey, B. (2017). *Seven interesting facts about Fyodor Dostoyevsky* [Blog post]. Accessed at https://blog.bookstellyouwhy.com/seven-interesting-facts-about-fyodor-dostoyevsky on March 29, 2019.

Kanter, R. M. (2006). *Confidence: How winning streaks and losing streaks begin and end.* New York: Three Rivers Press.

Kotter, J. P. (1996). *Leading change.* Boston: Harvard Business School Press.

Kotter, J. P. (2008). *A sense of urgency.* Boston: Harvard Business School Press.

Kotter, J. P., & Cohen, D. S. (2002). *The heart of change: Real-life stories of how people change their organizations.* Boston: Harvard Business School Press.

Kouzes, J. M., & Posner, B. Z. (2006). *A leader's legacy.* San Francisco: Jossey-Bass.

Kouzes, J. M. & Posner, B. Z. (2011). *Credibility.* San Francisco: Jossey-Bass.

Kouzes, J. M., & Posner, B. Z. (2012). *The leadership challenge: How to make extraordinary things happen in organizations* (5th ed.). San Francisco: Jossey-Bass.

Lindblom, C. E. (1959). The science of "muddling through." *Public Administration Review, 19*(2), 79–88.

Loschert, K. (2016, June 18). The suspension effect: Exclusionary discipline practices increase high school dropout rates and cost the nation billions in lost tax revenue, according to the Center for Civil Rights Remedies. *Straight A's Newsletter, 16*(13). Accessed at https://all4ed.org/articles/the-suspension-effect-exclusionary-discipline-practices-increase-high-school-dropout-rates-and-cost-the-nation-billions-in-lost-tax-revenue-according-to-the-center-for-civil-rights-remedies on March 26, 2019.

Magolda, P. M. (2005). Proceed with caution: Uncommon wisdom about academic and student affairs partnerships. *About Campus, 9*(6), 16–21.

Mankins, M., & Garton, E. (2017). *Time, talent, energy: Overcome organizational drag and unleash your team's productive power.* Boston: Harvard Business Review Press.

Marzano, R. J., Warrick, P. B., Simms, J. A., & Heflebower, T. (2014). *A handbook for high reliability schools: The next step in school reform.* Bloomington, IN: Marzano Resources.

Musca, T. (Producer), & Menéndez, R. (Director). (1988). *Stand and deliver* [Motion picture]. United States: Warner Bros.

Naisbitt, J., & Aburdene, P. (1985). *Re-inventing the corporation: Transforming your job and your company for the new information society.* New York: Warner Books.

Nanus, B. (1992). *Visionary leadership: Creating a compelling sense of direction for your organization.* San Francisco: Jossey-Bass.

Neason, A. (2017). Does homework help? *ASCD Education Update, 59*(1).

Newmann, F. M., & Wehlage, G. G. (1995). *Successful school restructuring: A report to the public and educators.* Madison, WI: Center on Organization and Restructuring of Schools.

Newport, C. (2016, February 18). A modest proposal: Eliminate email. *Harvard Business Review.* Accessed at https://hbr.org/2016/02/a-modest-proposal -eliminate-email on April 2, 2019.

Pelletier, M. (n.d.) Considering district size when establishing your target audience. *MDR.* Accessed at https://mdreducation.com/2018/04/20/school -district-sizes-target-audience on March 27, 2019.

Peters, T. J., & Waterman, R. H., Jr. (1982). *In search of excellence: Lessons from America's best-run companies.* New York: Harper & Row.

Pfeffer, J., & Sutton, R. I. (2000). *The knowing-doing gap: How smart companies turn knowledge into action.* Boston: Harvard Business School Press.

Pfeffer, J., & Sutton, R. I. (2006). *Hard facts, dangerous half-truths, and total nonsense: Profiting from evidence-based management.* Boston: Harvard Business School Press.

Porath, C. (2016). *Mastering civility: A manifesto for the workplace.* New York: Grand Central.

Reeves, D. (2001). *Holistic accountability: Serving students, schools, and community.* Thousand Oaks, CA: Corwin Press.

Reeves, D. (2002). *The daily disciplines of leadership: How to improve student achievement, staff motivation, and personal organization.* San Francisco: Jossey-Bass.

Reeves, D. (2004). *Accountability for learning: How teachers and school leaders can take charge.* Alexandria, VA: Association for Supervision and Curriculum Development.

Reeves, D. (2006). *The learning leader: How to focus school improvement for better results.* Alexandria, VA: Association for Supervision and Curriculum Development.

Reeves, D. (2011a). *Elements of grading: A guide to effective practice.* Bloomington, IN: Solution Tree Press.

Reeves, D. (2011b). *Finding your leadership focus: What matters most for student results.* New York: Teachers College Press.

Reeves, D. (2014). *Accountability in action: A blueprint for learning organizations.* Boston: Houghton Mifflin Harcourt.

Reeves, D. (2015). *Inspiring creativity and innovation in K–12.* Bloomington, IN: Solution Tree Press.

Reeves, D. (2016a). *FAST grading: A guide to implementing best practices.* Bloomington, IN: Solution Tree Press.

Reeves, D. (2016b). *From leading to succeeding: The seven elements of effective leadership in education.* Bloomington, IN: Solution Tree Press.

Reeves, D. (in press). *Achieving equity and excellence: Immediate results from the lessons of high-poverty, high-success schools.* Bloomington, IN: Solution Tree Press.

Reeves, D., & Reeves, B. (2017). *The myth of the muse: Supporting virtues that inspire creativity.* Bloomington, IN: Solution Tree Press.

Sawyer, K. (2007). *Group genius: The creative power of collaboration.* New York: Basic Books.

Schaffer, R. H., & Thomson, H. A. (1992). Successful change programs begin with results. *Harvard Business Review, 70*(1), 80–89.

Schlechty, P. C. (2009). *Leading for learning: How to transform schools into learning organizations.* San Francisco: Jossey-Bass.

Schmoker, M. J. (2011). *Focus: Elevating the essentials to radically improve student learning* (2nd ed.). Alexandria, VA: Association for Supervision and Curriculum Development.

Senge, P. M. (1990). *The fifth discipline: The art and practice of the learning organization.* New York: Doubleday.

Senge, P. M., Kleiner, A., Roberts, C., Ross, R. B., & Smith, B. J. (1994). *The fifth discipline fieldbook: Strategies and tools for building a learning organization.* New York: Currency.

Shmoop Editorial Team. (2008, November 11). *Franklin D. Roosevelt (FDR) first 100 days.* Accessed at https://shmoop.com/franklin-d-roosevelt-fdr/first-100-days.html on May 21, 2017.

Sinek, S. (2009). *Start with why: How great leaders inspire everyone to take action.* New York: Penguin.

Tye, L. (2016). *Bobby Kennedy: The making of a liberal icon*. New York: Random House.

U.S. Geological Survey. (n.d.). *Kilauea*. Accessed at https://volcanoes.usgs.gov /volcanoes/kilauea/ on April 2, 2019.

Walenta, C. (2010). *Constitutional FAQ answer #87*. Accessed at https:// usconstitution.net/constfaq_q87.html on March 29, 2019.

Waterman, R. H., Jr. (1987). *The renewal factor: How the best get and keep the competitive edge*. New York: Bantam Books.

Waters, J. T., & Marzano, R. J. (2006, September). *School district leadership that works: The effect of superintendent leadership on student achievement* (Working paper). Denver, CO: Mid-continent Research for Education and Learning.

Weisinger, H., & Pawliw-Fry, J. P. (2015). *Performing under pressure: The science of doing your best when it matters most*. New York: Crown Business.

WestEd. (2000). *Teachers who learn, kids who achieve: A look at schools with model professional development*. San Francisco: Author.

Whitaker, T. (2012). *Shifting the monkey: The art of protecting good people from liars, criers, and other slackers*. Bloomington, IN: Solution Tree Press.

INDEX

Learning by Doing
Richard DuFour, Rebecca DuFour, Robert Eaker, Thomas W. Many, and Mike Mattos
The third edition of this comprehensive action guide includes new strategies, tools, and tips for transforming your school or district into a high-performing PLC.
BKF746

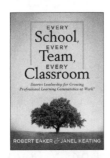

Every School, Every Team, Every Classroom
Robert Eaker and Janel Keating
The PLC journey begins with a dedication to ensuring the learning of every student. Using many examples and reproducible tools, the authors explain the need to focus on creating simultaneous top-down *and* bottom-up leadership. Learn how to grow PLCs by encouraging innovation at every level.
BKF534

From Leading to Succeeding
Douglas Reeves
Utilizing the crucial elements of effective leadership—purpose, trust, focus, leverage, feedback, change, and sustainability—education leaders can overcome any challenge. This book confronts leadership myths, offers guidance on best leadership practices, and provides the support leaders need to succeed.
BKF649

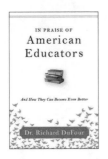

In Praise of American Educators
Richard DuFour
Explore the state of education today. The author establishes why contemporary American educators are the greatest generation in history and then presents specific steps policymakers and educators must take to transform American schools to meet student needs in the 21st century.
BKF702

Wait! Your professional development journey doesn't have to end with the last pages of this book.

We realize improving student learning doesn't happen overnight. And your school or district shouldn't be left to puzzle out all the details of this process alone.

No matter where you are on the journey, we're committed to helping you get to the next stage.

Take advantage of everything from **custom workshops** to **keynote presentations** and **interactive web and video conferencing**. We can even help you develop an action plan tailored to fit your specific needs.

Let's get the conversation started.

Call 888.763.9045 today.

SolutionTree.com